Planning

1990   1989   1988   1987   4   3   2   1

Library of Congress Cataloging-in-Publication Data

Peattie, Lisa Redfield.
  Planning, rethinking Ciudad Guayana.

  Bibliography: p.
  Includes index.
    1. New towns—Venezuela—Ciudad Guayana.
  2. City planning—Venezuela—Ciudad Guayana.
  I. Title.
  HT169.57.V42C586   1987   3071.7'68'098763   86-30789
  ISBN 0-472-10085-8 (alk. paper)
  ISBN 0-472-08069-5 (pbk. : alk. paper)

Cover photograph from *Planning Urban Growth and Regional
Development: The Experiences of the Guayana Program of Venezuela,* edited
by Lloyd Rodwin and Associates. Copyright © 1969 by The
Massachusetts Institute of Technology.

Illustration credits:
Figures 1, 4, 5, 6, and 7 courtesy of Wilhelm von Moltke.
Figures 2 and 3 reprinted from Corporación Venezolana de
Guayana, División de Estudios, Planificación e Investigación,
Ciudad Guayana Plan de Desarrollo Urbano (Caracas: CVG, n.d.), 14, 10.

The dream of reason did not take power into account.

Paul Starr, *The Social Transformation of American Medicine*

Acknowledgments

Many people have contributed to this enterprise. Lloyd Rodwin, Wilhelm von Moltke, Alexander Ganz, and William A. Porter were all major actors in the drama and subsequently gave me material, let themselves be interviewed at length, and read pieces of the manuscript in draft. William A. Doebele, another participant in the project, read and carefully criticized a whole first draft. John Thorkelson, another participant who read and commented on the manuscript, helped me especially in deepening my understanding of the economic planning. Martin Rein was not among this group of participants, but he also read and helpfully commented on chapters in draft. Later, John Forester and Peter Marris provided long and thoughtful comments on the manuscript, which pushed me to look at certain issues further. Other people who contributed in major ways were: John and Leticia MacDonald, Susan Vogeler, Andres Chemello, Claudio Brun, Johanna Glass de Lopes, Diane Dunlop, Elisenda Vila, Lucia Pinedo, and Marisela Montoliu. The suggestions by María-Pilar García, who has herself written extensively on the project, were especially helpful.

This is clearly a very opinionated book, and no one should hold these people responsible for it.

Contents

Introduction

This book has been growing for twenty years, really—ever since I went to Venezuela on two weeks notice to be part of the Joint Center for Urban Studies team planning Ciudad Guayana and stayed for two and a half years. Almost exactly a year into the project I wrote to one of the directors of the Joint Center about the interesting book that could be written "about the project itself." This book, I said,

> would be a kind of case history of a technical assistance project, with secondarily and tentatively perhaps some attempt to generalize from the one case. The book . . . would not be exactly "a history" . . . it would be more a description of several different views of reality with an analysis of the factors in the situation of each perceiving group which select for each a set of relevant realities. . . . This description might turn out to consist in part of several histories—i.e., the history of the project from the point of view of the Venezuelan staff of the CVG [Corporación Venezolana de Guayana] in Caracas . . . from the point of view of the chamber of commerce types in San Félix, from the point of view of the Joint Center, . . . etc. It would consist further of a description and analysis of the social relationship between these various groups, and the effect of each group and its point of view on the others.[1]

This is not that book, but it is something like that book, just as I am not the person who wrote the letter but a person something like the one who wrote the letter. Even if I could still get all those histories—now lost—I've had twenty years to think it over, and while I don't disagree with my younger self, the material has become part of some larger structures. Besides, the whole intellectual climate is different. Whatever happened to Progress through Planning? In fact, what happened to Progress?

Reality became different for me even in writing the book. After twenty years thinking about the project, reading the various studies and commentaries, teaching about it, writing about it, plus two trips back, roughly a decade apart, it seemed to me I knew the story. The book seemed to me a task of finding a form for what I knew. But it wasn't like that at all. The book repeatedly surprised me. I found things out, writing about them. This was not because I found new facts; it was because I thought about facts in a different way. Writing, I observed myself as involved in the social construction of reality, even as I tried to understand planning as an enterprise in the construction of reality.

Reality is both thought and action, and planning sits on the joint between thought and action and plays with their interrelations.

When I agreed to go to Venezuela I did so partly because I had been feeling dissatisfied with the conceptual vocabulary of anthropology. It seemed to be constructed for talking about continuations and not at all well adapted for talking about change. The interesting subjects got flattened out in the language of anthropology. I had been wanting to locate in some rapidly changing city where I would be driven to develop a different vocabulary. But I had thought of this as another vocabulary of description: a conceptualization of change. What I found in Guayana was passion, intention, and struggle. The world became politicized for me. Writing became discussion and argument. The anthropology of description would never satisfy me again.

Trained in the anthropological tradition of fieldwork and participant observation, it seemed reasonable to take up residence on "the site." We were a family, my architect husband and myself and four children, so we bought a house. It was a squatter shack, with whitewashed earth walls and a sheet metal roof facing out at the Orinoco. A family with both parents working for the Guayana Project and children in the local schools, living in a neighborhood where walls were thin and life an endless struggle, we began to make many kinds of connections with the people of the city. The first week we were there we helped a group of neighbors dig trenches for a water line that would bring water to twelve public taps—some days, some hours. I discussed local politics in the coffee shop on the plaza. We were taken to swim at the club of the Orinoco Mining Company, played checkers in the Basque restaurant down the road, attended community meetings, went to the outdoor movies at the Iron Mines camp.

Living on "the site" I became intoxicated by the energy unleashed by the development process. I had been brought up in a family of WASP intellectuals to downplay a concern with material things. Now, in a city of hustlers, for the first time I understood the enormous idealism contained in the vision of material progress. A working-class Venezuelan in dusty chinos showed me where his neighbors were making a school and said, "I have had a historic life." He went on to explain what he meant by that; he had grown up in a barter economy on the coast, gone to the mining camps, and was now seeing the coming of industry, "the future of the worker." As I listened, I knew that he was telling me something important.

Living on the site, while the main planning team was based in Caracas, meant that our experiences of the city differed from those of the other team members. It made for a different perspective and for different commitments. That was all according to plan: the anthropologist was hired to interpret "the people" to "the planners," so the people's characteristics and needs could be incorporated into the plan. But the go-between role was frustrating. The project was, after all, intended to achieve "national goals." The people living at the site were in the present; the city was in the future. The planners were sensitive to the needs of the big companies they wanted to attract; the needs of my neighbors would have to yield to the big strategy.

Two events symbolically framed my understanding. Our stay in the city had begun with a community work party to build a water line for the neighborhood. It ended with a different neighborhood project: a piece of sabotage directed at the building of a waste pipe that would carry sewage from a new middle-income urbanization onto our beach.[2] In the first project, I helped dig and helped serve food at the picnic that celebrated completion of the line. This time, I made coffee for the saboteurs.

Even as all this was happening, I recognized the role I was playing as a recurrent one in applied anthropology. In 1963 I wrote:

> The anthropologist speaks of the Wog point of view to the planners, and is to some degree identified by the other project members as the spokesman of the Wogs and as that odd body who does not seem to mind living among the natives. Thus he comes to develop himself, in his own psychological orientation, a kind of representative-client relationship to the people he is studying. He becomes committed to the group of people who are—in the original job description—his "subjects" of study. The situation in which he works is, further, characteristically one of disparity of power, in which that group to which he has come to feel committed appear as underdogs. Thus it happens often that the anthropologist comes to press the interests of the natives to the planners or administrators.[3]

My characteristically anthropological commitment to the underdog was facilitated in this situation by the fact that the people of the site, as a group, were committed to values very congenial to an American liberal. They had at all social levels, and especially perhaps at the bottom where the underdog phenomenon could come into play, that sense of being part of history, of being involved in processes of "nation making," "building the future," "building a people," which had become so exciting to me. The people of the site saw the planning and development agency not as the agent of this historic development but as a particular institution with special interests. I came to concur in this point of view. Thus I came to an identification with "the people" as my immediate reference group, as underdogs, and as in some sense the agents of historic transformation.

When, after I came back to the States, I wrote a book about the project, it was this vision that I wanted to represent. I wanted to represent the city as it appeared from the bottom and as a process of historic social change in which the basic force at work was the self-transforming energy of persons.

In the chapters that follow, I have tried to go back to something like the original vision of a "case history of a technical assistance project" focusing on "a description of several different views of reality": their origins and their consequences. Here I must try to put my own representation of the situation and of the planning process beside those of others. But this is not to claim some newfound objectivity. This is an argument also, advocacy in an enlarged and generalized form. This way of telling the story is one version among possible versions. After all, every telling represents a way of seeing. We see from where we stand; and why would we look unless we care about how the story comes out?

Notes

1. Lisa Peattie, letter to Martin Myerson, February 12, 1963.
2. See Lisa Redfield Peattie, "The Sewer Controversy: A Case History," chap. 7 in *The View from the Barrio* (Ann Arbor: University of Michigan Press, 1968), 71–90.
3. Lisa Peattie, "What to Do with Your Anthropologist" (Memorandum, November 1963).

Chapter 1

A Planned City

While we often speak of the need for planning, we know at the same time that a number of planned cities are just awful. Indeed, there is a group of very well known planned cities that, although widely separated in space and produced by nations with sharply differing cultures and politics, share certain strikingly unappealing characteristics. Brasília, Chandigarh, and Islamabad are particularly notable instances of the genre: cities of monumental buildings rendered sterile in effect because of the antiseptically orderly character of their setting; cities of the most rigorous separation of classes, which typically extends to excluding the poor altogether from the areas covered by planning controls; cities that seem unadapted to pedestrians, small enterprises, the modest, and the domestic.

Brazilians used to like to tell a story about a visitor to Brasília whose belt breaks. He is depicted going desperately from place to place holding up his pants in a city that offers no convenient shopping facilities at the local or neighborhood level.

In addition to such stories, there is by now a literature of criticism on these cities, of which Epstein's *Brasília: Myth and Reality* and Madhu Sarin's book on Chandigarh are two notable examples.[1] But so far as I know, these critiques always center around a concept of flawed planning. The planners misjudged; the planners were unsympathetic to the needs of the masses. I propose here to explore another way of thinking about the similar obnoxiousness of these planned cities: that it results from the nature and functions of central planning itself. I propose to explore this possibility via the story of another well-known planned city in Venezuela with which I myself had some years of involvement in its early days.

Ciudad Guayana, the city of this story, differs sharply from Brasília, Chandigarh, and Islamabad in not being a government capital. It was proposed not as a seat of and monument to government, but as an industrial growth pole. In Brasília or Chandigarh, the city's business is government; in Ciudad Guayana, government's business was industry. The announced purpose of the city was economic growth and the decentralization of development away from the capital. Nevertheless, there are certain similarities between this city and the three capitals mentioned earlier. Like them, it is characterized by strikingly large buildings in an otherwise sparsely developed area. Like them, it excludes the poor from the area of planning controls. Like them, it has an awkward, inhuman quality as a place to live.

Can it be that planning is not the way to a better environment after all?

If planning is the way to better cities, Ciudad Guayana should have turned out splendidly. It was not only located at a dramatic natural site, with a rich collection of natural resources, it was planned by an international team of experts under a powerful independent agency with extensive legal powers and ample funding.

In a national magazine article on the planning of Ciudad Guayana, one of those most involved in organizing the project wrote in 1965:

In the lower Orinoco Valley of Venezuela, a new city is rising. Called Ciudad Guayana, this city is more than just another urban settlement; it is the focal point of an effort to establish the national economy of Venezuela on a broader and more stable basis than its present heavy dependence on petroleum.

As such the city of Guayana is perhaps one of the most ambitious and significant enterprises of its kind in the world today.[2]

In 1961, when Ciudad Guayana was founded, Venezuela was completing its third decade of petroleum-driven economic growth. A nation two-thirds rural in 1936 had become two-thirds urban and was still urbanizing rapidly. Oil—still in the hands of U.S. companies—accounted for 22 percent of the Venezuelan gross national product (GNP), two-thirds of Venezuelan government revenue, and 90 percent of foreign exchange. The democratically elected Betancourt government that came to power after the years of dictatorship announced as its major strategy that of "sowing the oil"—of using the oil royalties to build a permanent economic base. The Ciudad Guayana project was part of the national planning strategy that was the outcome of the oil boom, and it was financed by the oil revenues.

The new city was to be at the junction of the Orinoco and Caroní rivers in the south of Venezuela. Eight degrees off the equator, sea level, the area was hot and dry. The existing urban settlements there lacked a phone system, a public library, a theater or a university, and even, to a great extent, piped running water! More important, in many ways, it was an airline journey or a twelve-hour drive from Caracas, the glittering city where money and power and the contacts to get more of them were concentrated. But it had a dramatic natural site (two rivers, and a spectacular waterfall) and a rich collection of natural resources (hydroelectric power, iron, bauxite). Two U.S. companies, subsidiaries of U.S. Steel and Bethlehem Steel, were already mining iron in the area and shipping it out from company towns in the area of the proposed city. The Orinoco River provided access to cheap water transport for the heavy ore. The Venezuelan government owned and managed a dam and hydroelectric plant and was completing a steel mill. There were thus ore, energy, transportation, and the beginning of basic industry.

The program for developing these resources was backed up with both money and power. The development of the region and the planning of the new city were under the charge of a powerful development agency, the Corporación Venezolana de Guayana (CVG), responsible only to the president of Venezuela. Its head, Colonel Alfonzo Ravard, was a military officer, an engineer with an already-established reputation as an administrator in the region. The agency's control over land—not only to regulate use but to allocate through sale or lease—superseded the powers of the local municipal government.

Furthermore, in 1961 the CVG signed an agreement with the Joint Center for Urban Studies of the Massachusetts Institute of Technology and Harvard University for research and technical assistance in regional development and in planning the city, which made available a great deal of high-powered professional expertise. The contract provided for a total of $883,700 worth of professional services over three years.[3] In July of 1964, a two-year extension was signed providing for an additional $1,081,200.[4] The CVG also funded a large staff of Venezuelan counterparts in the planning enterprise.

Twenty years later, there is a city of around 350,000 people where the planners drew plans for one—but one rather different from the planners' dream.

On the eastern side of the Caroní River there had been in 1962 the rather raggle-taggle municipal center of San Félix with its plaza and market. Now there is a vast proliferation of shantytown settlements spreading south and east of the plaza, once a comfortably shabby shaded space, now an expanse of concrete.

On the west side of the Caroní, the location of the steel mill and the modern U.S. Steel company town called Puerto Ordaz, there are commercial office blocks in several scattered groupings and the development agency's own monumental building. There are also a number of residential developments for the middle- and higher-income groups. Many of these consist of high-rise apartment buildings standing scattered about the vast sunbaked spaces. Because during the oil boom the developers overbuilt for a very small high-income market, when I visited in 1982 I was told there were eight thousand vacant apartments. A particularly luxurious development, built to house the staff of the steel mill, was too expensive even for those rather well-paid persons and was one of the empty projects.

One problem is that the major industries that were to make the city an economic growth pole are in terrible trouble: a source not of industrial dynamism and of national income but of debt and managerial concern. When oil prices suddenly soared in 1973, more than ten billion dollars of Venezuela's new OPEC riches went into Guayana,[5] largely into a fourfold expansion of the steel mill and the enlargement of productive capacity in electricity and aluminum. But the implementing agencies turned out to lack the managerial capacity to execute the ambitious projects. While the city's facilities were strained to the point of crisis, the industrial projects brought accusations of patronage and mismanagement. Meanwhile, even as oil revenues fell, the world markets for steel and aluminum dropped sharply.

But the problems of the city are not simply those of running out of money. This is not the city that the planners intended, even at reduced scale. In 1986, I am told, the vacant apartments have been filled and the city is growing. But what kind of a city is it? The planners had concerned themselves with issues of economic efficiency, amenity, social equity, and community. The city as it has evolved is conspicuously lacking on all four counts.

It lacks efficiency. Three-quarters of the population live at one end of a lineal city, and the major industries and two-thirds of the jobs are located at the other end; thus, the majority of the working population must commute daily the length of the city. They must make the commute across a classic bottleneck: a double bridge over the river that separates the two sections. This distribution of population is not at all that which was planned.

Although specific predictions varied, all the planners, whether calculating by hand or by computer, proposed that "in the long run . . . residential growth would move westward from Puerto Ordaz in a broad band toward the steel mill, leaving only a minority of the population in San Félix."[6] The situation is at present reversed, since nearly three-quarters of the population live to the east in San Félix.

Both halves of the city lack amenity. The eastern part of the city, in which the working class lives, consists of a series of shantytown settlements. Streets are cheaply paved, if at all, and lack adequate drainage. In 1983 a study found that only a third of households in this sector were connected to the city water system.[7] Only 60 percent of the elementary school age population and 12 percent of the older youth were enrolled in school; although all schools were functioning on double shifts, the system simply lacked capacity.[8]

Puerto Ordaz, on the other side of the river where the privileged classes live, in contrast to the shantytowns of the east, is characterized by an awkward and unpleasant luxury: high-rise apartment buildings scattered widely apart, without pedestrian access, without trees and gardens, and with a deficiency of places for meeting and collective amusement.

The city lacks equity. Per capita, the development agency in 1977 had invested in the privileged Puerto Ordaz part thirty-nine times what it had invested in the working-class part[9]—and it is apparent to any casual glance.

The city lacks community. A 1983 report from the urban development agency points to the numerous factors which create a strong social segregation within the urban area: (1) natural barriers, especially the river, (2) the sharp segregation of use brought about by zoning, (3) the socioeconomic homogeneity of each residential area, and (4) the relative autonomy of the state-owned industrial enterprises. "Ciudad Guayana," the study says, "more than any other city, may be conceived of as a group of communities and a stratification of social groups."[10]

It is not only that there is no single center that serves as a point of identification for all the citizens (or more accurately in this case, the inhabitants). More striking is the fact that after twenty years, no one but the planners themselves still think of it as a single city. Ciudad Guayana as an entity exists only in the publicity flyers of the development agency. If one is to purchase a ticket at the Caracas airport, the airline will not know what you are talking about if you ask for Ciudad Guayana; you may get a ticket to Puerto Ordaz, the iron-mining company town that existed before planning began. The telephone directory has a section for Puerto Ordaz, the west side of the river, and another, linked only by the same area code, for San Félix on the east side. Some think of three settlements, adding to San Félix and Puerto Ordaz an industrial district called Matanzas.[11]

Of those who were involved in the planning effort back in the sixties, most have left the scene; the Americans, of course, have mainly returned to the States. Many have not even been back to visit. The chief economist of the project, while based in Boston, is an exception, for he was brought back by the development agency in the mid-seventies to work on the expansion made possible by the oil boom.

His view of the outcome of the project centers on the role of the city for national economic objectives:

The Guayana program has achieved its basic goals. An urban-industrial hydro-power center has been established and is thriving and expanding, albeit with growing pains, rough edges and missteps. Population of Ciudad Guayana has risen from 4,000 in 1960 to 300,000 plus in the 1980s and is growing. The industrial base continues to expand; a new bauxite mine and ore processing plant are currently being brought on stream and the Guayana is again proving useful. In this time of declining oil revenues, devaluation and import restrictions, the Guayana region is serving the national economy well.[12]

The chief urban designer of the Joint Center team, Wilhelm von Moltke, visited the city for a few days in February of 1981 and even more briefly in early 1984. On both occasions he was delighted by the good results of at least one of the design team's ideas: that of laying out urbanizations in a cul-de-sac pattern with loop access roads surrounding central open spaces. Proposed by the designers as a way of creating green spaces and of building community at the neighborhood level, the scheme was subsequently abandoned in the face of criticism of its complexity and cost relative to more standard blocks. But in the experimental prototypes were the green areas and in at least one case a small community building! In other respects, however, the city was to von Moltke rather distressing. In 1981 he drafted a memorandum with his impressions for the CVG. He commended the "vitality of the city" but declared himself:

> very disappointed in the environmental quality of the Alta Vista Center, the absence of human scale, the lack of visual structure, the lack of integration of the many large elements, the lack of concern for the pedestrian, the lack of landscaping, street furniture and other amenities.

He saw the "miscellaneous high-rise apartment buildings . . . in most inappropriate locations" and the "continued development of residential areas east and south-east of San Félix [which] extends the journey-to-work." He felt strongly that a height limit on buildings should have been imposed.[13]

Lloyd Rodwin revisited the city in 1977 with his wife. In the course of his trip he noted the "disastrous" decision on the part of the agency to sell off the land in the center of the city. "The values and the rents from this land," he wrote in a letter to the president of the CVG, "are essential for recapturing a reasonable share of the infrastructure investments.[14] In a more philosophical mood, a few years later, he observed:

> It turned out to be a tougher job than we thought. It was harder to find the right people. People who looked good would turn out to be disasters. There were constraints which the planning team didn't recognize.[15]

The city did not turn out as planned. One problem, of course, was the disappearance of the resource base when oil prices dropped. But this is not the whole story. There would not have been eight thousand vacant apartments in 1981 if the oil boom had continued—although it seems likely that even with the oil boom not all that building would have found a market. But the inefficiency, inequity, and lack of community characterizing the city were there before the oil boom and during the boom as they are now. Even during the boom, oil wealth did not seem to be producing a city that was agreeable to live in; on the contrary, there were protests from both the planners and the citizens as to the "crisis" produced for the city by oil-supported industrial expansion.

No, we must see the present problematic city not simply as the outcome of resource shifts; it is also the outcome of planning. The planners, their way of working, and the way that working process interacted with the other things that were going on in the city and in Venezuela constitute the roots of the present. The city was not planned as it is, but the city is the outcome of planning. The planning process helped make it what it is.

One way of explaining the undesirable outcome of the city is as planning messed up; people and institutions failed to obey the plan. The planners were unable to enforce their plans and thus to realize their dream. Rodwin's 1965 paper warned about the difficulties in implementing planning controls:

Attracted by the prospect of jobs, poor migrants invade the area, put up makeshift shelters and exacerbate the problem of organizing land uses and public services. Most costs tend to be high, almost no amenities exist and living conditions are bleak. Understandably enough, the inhabitants become impatient with "fancy" long-range plans and delays; they grumble about the neglect of their immediate needs and care little if these needs do not fit the priorities or the plans. Up to a point their views can be slighted or ignored, but this is always dangerous. It is hardly surprising that the new city rarely measures up to the original dreams of its planners.[16]

A simpler version of this argument was provided by a Venezuelan economist with the project whom I met again, after twenty years, when I revisited the development agency's offices in January 1982. I asked him how he thought the city had turned out. "Well," he said, "no matter how well they plan it, people keep moving in and messing it up."

This way of looking at the problem was clearly present from the beginning of the planning process. Indeed, the desire to keep people from moving in and messing up the planned city was, it will be seen, a basic reason for the separation between rich and poor, and the contrast between the settlements on the east and west of the river.

A second explanation also departs from the failure of the planners to control the actual processes of urban growth, but this time puts the blame on the planners. The planning process was too rigid. What was wanted, it is argued, was not so much a plan or final design, but a program for directing and channeling urban growth. This way of viewing the issue, like the preceding one, was also present from the beginning, put forward in a succession of consultant memoranda from the early days.

The more fundamental problem is to view the plan not as a static design but as a path of growth.[17]

Accept the idea that we should be making a plan for the nature,
rate, quantity and quality of urban change and a plan for the
development process rather than a plan for some static future
state (which will never occur in just that form).[18]

Any expectation that the ultimate appearance of the city will
be like the planning team's initial blueprint will be doomed to
disappointment. . . . One of the main factors that will control
the city's future pattern will not be what is put into the blueprint as much as what will be imposed by rancho (i.e., squatter
settlement) movements.[19]

The comments are surely justified; the production of a plan,
in the sense of a set of visually displayed decisions as to the locations of various activities in some future state of the city, was
not sufficient to direct the activities to those places. Nor could
the planners stop various institutional and personal actors from
doing what they wanted to do, rather than what the planners
wanted them to do. Even in the early days, when the development agency had decreed a freeze on all construction until such
time as the plan should have been developed, squatters continued
to put up their shacks and commercial developers continued to
construct buildings counter to plan; Sears was building a six-story
office building while the planners debated the nature of the commercial center elsewhere in which Sears was to be the prime tenant. A focus on the plan as locational map did little to organize
a process which could have negotiated such decisions.

A third view is that the planners were snobs. They were unable
to plan realistically for the development of the city, since to do
so would have been to recognize and provide for the needs of a
mass of poor and low-status people with whom they did not
wish to be identified. Snobbery identified the proper outcome of
planning with the urban settings appropriate for high-income
people, the "modern" with the expensive. Snobbery kept the

workers at one end of the city, away from both the industrial jobs to which they would have to commute and the urbanizations of the elite.

Again, there is evidence for an endemic snobbery, both among the planners and among others of the citizenry. When I revisited the city twenty years after my first arrival and asked my cab driver what he thought of the planning, he compared San Félix, the working-class side of the river, to Puerto Ordaz, the upper-income part of the city: "San Félix is terribly planned—all shantytowns; Puerto Ordaz—that's well planned."

These three perspectives are not mutually exclusive. Indeed, I believe that they are all in various ways true. The planning process was one that focused on formal order and on the production of a somewhat statically conceived spatial plan. There was little use of the planning process as one of interacting with, and thus coming to mobilize and direct, the actions of local people. The plan was indeed altered by the initiatives of private actors, not only the squatters whom Abrams saw as shaping the urbanization pattern but also some large corporate investors who put their buildings where they chose, rather than where the plans had proposed. And indeed a strain of unrecognized, perhaps even unconscious, social snobbery in the planners responded to the demand outside the planning office for "nice" neighborhoods and a "high standard" city.

Furthermore, the three interpretations are interrelated. The social separation of the planners from the people of the site, the institutional basis of the attitudes we call snobbery, helped to drive the planning process toward formalism. The formalism, in turn, made for a process that left "implementation" for a second stage of consideration, rather than using planning to develop the social supports for a proposed development path. This process certainly left an opening for unplanned actors to develop counter to the plan.

I wish to propose, here, a fourth interpretation. This, too, does not exclude the others. It constitutes, rather, a way of thinking about the relationships between the others and between the social roots of the planning enterprise. Here, planning will be thought of as a kind of social ritual, the function of which is to legitimize government activities that, if frankly described, would arouse conflict and dissent. The so-called mistakes in planning Ciudad Guayana may be understood as the working out of certain irreducible conflicts in the real unstated goals of the project, issues that were fuzzed over by the way in which the objectives of the city were described and the way in which the planning was carried out. Planning a growth pole meant reorganizing the environment for large corporations. The planners could not have taken the local businessmen and residents into the process without diluting this overriding objective. Therefore, they left them outside. Planning was a way of shifting power and resources toward large corporate bodies. But to make this explicit would have been to threaten the political legitimacy of the government that executed the policy, and which depended on voter support. If planning had been thought of in terms of process, all this would have been quite visible. Thought of as urban design and economic targets, it became a collective product: The City Plan and The Planned City.

The planners were very idealistic people. They believed in what they were doing. One of the functions of the planning process was to construct the planning activity in a form that enabled the planners themselves to feel they were serving an essentially noble purpose. The design focus served to convert the city into a kind of monument to the idea of progress, an ideological construction within which private gain could be thought of as social progress and the general good. The attention to "good design" and values of "amenity," thought of as there for the general enjoyment, made it possible to think of an undivided community interest in the outcome of the planning process. Underlying uneasinesses about class divisions and income contrasts were addressed through a focus on physical centers: neighborhood centers, the city center as "the heart of the city." Finally, the organization of an interdisciplinary team, including an anthropologist, made it possible to think of planning as addressing social issues and, indeed, as a technique of liberal reform.

In the following chapters I look at how these processes have worked themselves out in the planning of Ciudad Guayana, and attempt to draw some generalizations as to the nature of planning and urban design as professional practice and as instruments of control and distribution.

Notes

1. David G. Epstein, *Brasília—Plan and Reality: A Study of Planned and Spontaneous Urban Development* (Berkeley: University of California Press, 1983); Madhu Sarin, *Urban Planning in the Third World: The Chandigarh Experience* (New York: Mansell Publishing, 1982).

2. Lloyd Rodwin, "Ciudad Guayana: A New City," *Scientific American,* September 1965, 122–23.

3. "Memorandum of Agreement between the Corporación Venezolana de Fomento hereinafter Sometimes Referred to as the 'Corporación' and the Massachusetts Institute of Technology hereinafter Sometimes Referred to as 'M.I.T.' " (1961, Mimeographed).

4. "Memorandum of Agreement between the Corporación Venezolana de Guayana and the Massachusetts Institute of Technology, March 1964" (Mimeographed).

5. Jackson Diehl, "Venezuela's Force-Fed Industrial Center Goes on a Crash Diet," *Washington Post,* March 4, 1983, sec. A.

6. Anthony Penfold, "Urban Transportation," in *Planning Urban Growth and Regional Development: The Experience of the Guayana Program of Venezuela,* by Lloyd Rodwin et al. (Cambridge: MIT Press, 1969), 187–88.

7. CVG, Ministerio del Desarrollo Urbano, *Ciudad Guayana XXI: Logros, problemas y oportunidades, una síntesis del diagnostico* (Caracas: CVG, 1983), 9.

8. Ibid., 14.

9. Claude Brun M., *Ciudad Guayana más allá de 1980* (Caracas: CVG, División de Ingeniería y Construcción, Departamento de Planeamiento Urbano, 1979), 9.
10. CVG, Ministerio del Desarrollo Urbano, *Ciudad Guayana XXI,* 7.
11. Ibid., 9.
12. Alexander Ganz, letter to author, May 26, 1986.
13. "Impressions of Ciudad Guayana from a Visit on February 25, 1981" (Typed memorandum from Willo von Moltke to General Alfonzo Ravard).
14. Lloyd Rodwin, letter to Dr. Argenis Gamboa, president of the CVG, February 2, 1977.
15. Lloyd Rodwin, interview with author, April 5, 1983.
16. Rodwin, "Ciudad Guayana," 122.
17. William Alonso, "Report Concerning Some Aspects of the Projected Guayana City" (Joint Center Guayana Project, Memorandum A-6, July 1962), 28.
18. Robert B. Mitchell, "Observations and Recommendations after Visit to Caracas, January 28–February 3, 1962" (Joint Center Guayana Project, Memorandum A-4, February 1962), 15.
19. Charles Abrams, "Report on the Development of Ciudad Guayana in Venezuela" (Joint Center Guayana Project, Memorandum A-5, January 1962), 26.

Chapter 2

Models and Motivations

To the dispassionate eye of a disengaged tourist, there was not too much to see at the site of Ciudad Guayana in 1961. There were the two rivers and a certainly spectacular waterfall; in the vicinity were a number of the works of man—an undistinguished commercial-center town, a corporate company town, and a number of government projects: the still-unfinished steel mill, the dam, the hydroelectric plant.

But people concerned with Ciudad Guayana were not disengaged tourists, and they saw the place with eyes that were anything but dispassionate. A set of passionate ideas, ideological constructions, in which planning was to play a major part, bathed the scene in the light of future expectations and social and personal commitment.

At the time, it appeared that the various actors on the scene shared a common vision of progress and of the means to attain it, even while they argued over the proper order of actions and the sharing of advantages.

In retrospect, certain differences in vision become apparent. The various actors—the CVG top administration, the American and Venezuelan planners, the engineers, the local business elite and politicians, the ordinary citizens—did not, it turns out, have quite the same sorts of future in mind. But it is important to realize that they very largely felt as though they did; while they argued about what was to be done, they shared in the exhilarating sense of being part of a historic social process.

When the project began, in 1961, Venezuela was a nation that

had only recently been transformed by thirty years of a U.S.-
dominated oil boom. Oil prosperity brought roads, schools, radios, and mass literacy. Oil transformed the population itself;
from 1940 to 1960 the death rate dropped by half; by the sixties
the population of Venezuela was growing at a rate of around 4
percent a year, and 42 percent of the people were under fourteen
years of age. Oil prosperity attracted a massive European immigration, and the immigrants, in turn, became a source of skills
and enterprise. Oil and the spending that went with it brought
about an enormous transfer of population from the country to
the city. A nation largely rural a few decades before was rapidly
becoming a nation of city dwellers.

In this period, as Venezuela was consolidating a national iden-
tity around material progress, no region could have been more
appropriate symbolically for a target of development than was
the Guayana. In literature and in popular imagination it had an
established place as the romantic frontier. It was an area of cattle
raising and mining; there once had been a great gold boom, and
people still recurrently rushed to pan for diamonds in the Caroní
River. The Orinoco, its upper boundary, tapped unmapped jun-
gles and gathered waters into one of the world's greatest rivers.
To the south, the road ended at the foot of the great escarpment
of the Grand Savanna in a little settlement where cold beer and
American apples were for sale in the cooler of the general store.
The very landscape seemed to read potential.

The oil that was the basis of the recent economic transformation of Venezuela was, it may be argued, also the basis of
democratic government in Venezuela, for it was in part the spread
of communications—roads, literacy—and of popular aspirations
that brought the elected Betancourt government into power. But
it was an elected government that was weaker in political organization than in economic power. A technocratic, or planning,
approach to issues was politically convenient. Electoral government was new and fragile. Democracy had had a trial run from

1945 to 1948, and its leaders knew from experience how easily they could be overthrown. Rather than press at once for radical reforms, the new Betancourt government devoted itself to building coalitions among a broad spectrum of social and political groups. Political caution suggested a strategy that oil resources made possible: a focus on growth rather than distribution. Technical solutions involving the application of more resources instead of restructuring the institutions seemed the appropriate path. The rising tide that floats all boats would make possible consensus and political stability.

Furthermore, there was an extraordinary congruence between the Venezuelan experience and the dominant vision of the planning technocracy. Development planning of the period involved a belief in the power of heavy industrial investment to alter radically the structure of the economy; in effect, it was argued that sufficient capital could produce almost instant modernization. It fitted the Venezuelan experience with oil; the Caracas superhighways and high-rise apartments were visual proof of what money could do. Furthermore, the style of American planning for development in the less developed countries was, in this period, distinctly oriented toward big ticket goals. Modern steel mills in the jungle and huge hydroelectric projects on untamed rivers both appealed to the imagination of clients like Colonel Ravard and were legitimized in the perspectives of American-trained economists.

Something more in the dominant ideology of Progress needs to be expressed, although it is harder to put a finger on it: the extraordinary power of the American image of fully developed, mature, consumer-society capitalism. The American presence was, of course, everywhere in Venezuela, in the companies that dominated economic life, in the well-watered lawns and trim houses of the American managerial staff, in the American films, and in the consumer goods that styled the forms of economic aspiration. The gloss of these images of progress, American-style, was of course intensified by the selectivity of what reached Venezuela: Americans in the companies were management, not the lower-grade workers; American company towns conveyed nothing of the decay of central cities in the United States; even the political processes of the United States were understood, by informants in Ciudad Guayana at least, as textbook democracy, not as the actual rough-and-tumble of the smoke-filled room and the political bargain. Along with a prickly-proud nationalism, Venezuelans seemed to have a tendency to derogate their own competence as a people and to look admiringly at the order, wealth, and power of the American enterprises that had taken root among them.

This made it less troubling—perhaps even an attraction—that a development plan might be designed to fit the needs of the already-developed industrial economies, and especially that of the United States. The American earth-moving machinery would build the city, and American corporations would be courted as potential participants in the city.

Oil revenues made a Venezuelan elite that thought readily of importing modernity. Well-to-do Venezuelans were conspicuous spenders in a nation that came to import most of its consumer goods. They imported clothes, cars, toasters, radios, even pines for Christmas trees. It seemed natural to such an elite to import technical skill: to buy planning.

In this context, it seemed only natural for the CVG planners to focus on developing Guayana by *attracting* already-developed enterprises and already-skilled technicians rather than stressing the *transformation* of what and who was already on the site. This way of approaching the problem will be documented in what follows; what is important to understand first is that it was almost unquestioned, shaped as it was by powerful economic logic, by class interest, and as a reflection of a deeply felt although not fully articulated ideology of progress that the planners shared with most Venezuelans at all levels of society.

The CVG was an independent national agency, responsive directly to the president of the republic. Its economic program had the following broad objectives.

a) Decentralization of the national economy through the incorporation of a promising area in the interior of the country, creating and strengthening a pole of development.
b) Effective economic utilization of resources not previously exploited, and expansion of production of those already tapped, in line with the criteria of comparative advantage.
c) Industrial growth, especially in those branches which have proven to be the most dynamic in the economy.
d) Provision of stable and remunerative employment; contributing in an important way to betterment of living standards in the Eastern part of the country, and alleviating the demographic pressure in the States and the Territory which it comprises.
e) Contribution to the growth of total production and output per worker, both on a regional as well as a national scale.
f) Dispersion of the effect of development on other complementary economic sectors, through industrial linkages and growth induced by rising demand.
g) Favorable impact on the balance of payments, both through the reduction of certain types of external purchases through the substitution of imports, as well as an increase in foreign exchange earnings from new exports.[1]

The head of this agency, Colonel (later to become General) Ravard, was a graduate of the Massachusetts Institute of Technology. A political survivor, he had been, under the dictatorship of Pérez Jiménez, the head of the agency charged with developing electric power on the Caroní; when the dictator was overthrown he proceeded to consolidate a position of power under the new government. He had a reputation for "clean" technocratic administration.

His top managers, all men, were mainly in their early thirties, with strong ties of personal loyalty to Ravard and to each other. They were all graduates of the Caracas Jesuit school, ideologically close to the Catholic church, and active either in Opus Dei or the Movimiento Familiar Cristiano. None were active in party politics. All but two were independently wealthy.

The agency had already built one dam and power plant at the site of Ciudad Guayana, and now Ravard, as head of CVG, wanted to build a bigger one, upstream at Guri.

An American staff member who knew Ravard rather well saw the central issue for Ravard as being the legitimizing of the Guri Dam project. "Ravard liked electric power," he told me in January 1983.

> It was clean; it didn't employ many people. He was not too keen on the steel mill; there were all sorts of complications—labor problems. He wanted the World Bank *imprimatur* on Guri—not because Venezuela needed the money, but because if the World Bank gave the loan it made it a credible project. The early Bank report (on the project) said there was no question but that electricity could be produced cheaply there [at Guri] but where is the market? . . . When the World Bank team came again, he made sure that some Joint Center people were there. The second time they looked, they said "Yes, there is a market."

A major part of this market was in the production of aluminum. At least one economic consultant argued that since aluminum production employed very few workers and would require tariff protection to be competitive "it would not be a great loss to forego the aluminum plant in favor of some more labor intensive projects."[2] However, aluminum did constitute a large market for electric power. One of the Venezuelan planners summed it up: "Alfonzo [Ravard] wanted to justify the dam. The whole structure was set up to sell energy. When they found bauxite that was pure luck."[3]

The engineers of the CVG were, taken as a group, people whose commitment to the program was via building of projects. They saw the city planners as *espiritistas*—impractical idealists. The engineer in charge of the Urban Development Division told me in September 1963:

> If they would let us build, we could build the city in a month. There is no use doing extensive remodeling of San Félix. The people here themselves will replan it. We can have 250,000 educated people here in ten years. They will remodel the city.

Down at the site of the projected city, where some 45,000 people were living when the planning exercise began, the local government and local business elite—essentially a single group of people—had a perspective not very different from that of the engineers. They, too, wanted building: roads, water lines, sewers, new factories. The difference was that they saw the developments as stemming from initiatives that they themselves had taken, and they wanted to control and benefit from the outcomes rather than see power and profits absorbed by outsiders. They had a historic perspective, in which current developments were part of the romance of Guayana; among them were persons who kept books of clippings on the history and development of the region. They saw the steel mill as having been brought to their area by their political influence. They wanted the new works to nourish their commercial and real estate interests. They did not see a city to be created; for them, it was already present in embryo. They deeply resented what seemed to them a slow pace of CVG decision making: a way of working which appeared not as one which promoted development so much as retarding it. Particularly did the municipal government resent the preemption by the CVG of the municipal lands, traditionally a major source of revenue and political support.

In the words of the head of the local municipal council in May 1963:

> The people of Caracas who are there stuck to the air-conditioning—which they don't need, because they have a very nice climate—have no idea of San Félix. For instance, they will send an electoral commission suitable for a hamlet. They do not understand it is a little town—fifty thousand to eighty thousand people—with aspirations to be a city, with urban atmosphere. . . . There are plans, marvelous plans. Since 1957 they have been making plans—where the buildings will be, where the transportation networks will be. But when you want to put something someplace the municipal council can't do it—you have to ask the development agency which has its office not here but in a marvelous office in the Shell Building. They make plans and in a year or so they erase them to study and make another, erase to study and make another.
>
> The nucleus of San Félix is almost exclusively workers—based on the Orinoco Mining Company and Iron Mines company and the steel mill; the commerce and few industries revolve around the companies and the steel mill. When other possibilities come in sight they can't tell us where they can locate. Now they have out for bids a beautiful aqueduct, good for three million people. The municipal council has to keep opening wells. The tubes are perpetually getting choked with sand because of excessive suction on the inadequate wells. The council has to supply water to distant barrios by truck. San Félix needs five thousand hospital beds—it has about two hundred.
>
> It is the custom here to talk of the great river, of the magnificent waterfall, of the aluminum plant of Reynolds which

will provide aluminum for all Venezuela. But I think we must
talk here of the truth. We are suffering hunger, suffering thirst,
suffering difficulties.

Working-class residents of the city had none of the sense of
proprietorship of the local political-commercial elite, but their
attachment to the idea of material progress was, if anything, even
more intense. Some of the local leaders, coming out of the old
regional elite, spoke with regret of the old days when "families
were families" and the "better people" of the regional center still
further south held parlor musicales. But the working-class idea
of progress held none of these memories and reservations. "We
used to live in the darkness; now we are coming into the light,"
said an older man from the Delta, talking to me about the spread
of public schooling. Although the distribution of gains during the
oil boom had been terribly uneven, the boom had meant to the
people at the bottom of the Venezuelan social structure a tremendous opening up of new opportunities. The newly formed urban
working class, even with a quarter of them unemployed and
many more scraping out a marginal living in various sorts of
marginal activities, still had very great faith in the march of
progress. The fact that there were many strains of discontent did
not preclude an enormous optimism in Venezuela which was
probably nowhere stronger than in the frontier region of Guayana. When a sample of individuals in Guayana were asked in 1962
to forecast their situation five years hence, 77 percent said it would
be better and only 3 percent that it would be worse. There was
an extraordinary belief in the openness of Venezuelan society;
asked whether any capable person could become a civil servant,
a lawyer, the owner of a large or small enterprise, a high government employee, a high military official, or a high political
leader, in each category over 85 percent of respondents said yes.[4]
In Guayana workers even more than the well-to-do pointed
with pride and a degree of identification to such physical manifes-

tations of progress as the steel mill or the new dock in Ciudad Guayana.

The ideology embracing these several strands of energetic optimism was the idea of economic growth. It had its popular version among those formally uneducated migrants to the city who spoke to me about "progress," about "building the country," and "the future of the worker." It had its sophisticated version among the planners, with their investment programs and economic targets. In the early sixties, the ideas of development planning, the conceptualizations which Latins were later to denigrate as an ideology of *desarrollismo,* were still in very good standing among intellectuals. Thinking about consciously managed economic change had moved through an early phase of concern with "cultural barriers" and the sources of entrepreneurship to a set of ideas focusing very much on capital investment and a confidence in "leading sectors" which would pull the rest of the economy along in a march toward general societal progress. It had not yet become fashionable to ridicule the GNP as an indicator of the condition of societies. The international agencies had yet to experience their struggles with the ideas of "redistribution with growth"[5] and "basic needs strategies."[6]

In 1962 the American planners who arrived in Caracas to plan a new city and develop the Guayana region were very much engaged in discussing the ideas of Walter Rostow, whose *Stages of Economic Growth* represented a formulation of the prevailing development ideology in a form particularly gratifying to planners and other members of society's managerial elites. (Rostow's book, first published in 1960, went through thirteen printings by 1965.) Rostow's focus on "certain leading sectors . . . whose rapid rate of expansion plays an essential direct and indirect role in maintaining the overall momentum of the economy"[7] provided the rationale for an enthusiastic reception of large, corporate investors under any ownership and management—private or government, foreign or domestic. At the same time, the analysis provided a heroic role for elite leadership and societal management.

> Some men in the society must be able to manipulate and apply
> . . . modern science and cost-reducing inventions.
> Some other men in the society must be prepared to undergo
> the strain and risks of leadership; in bringing the flow of available inventions productively into the capital stock.
> Some other men in the society must be prepared to lend
> their money on long term, at high risk, to back the innovating entrepreneurs . . . in modern industry.
> And the population at large must be prepared to accept
> training for—and then to operate—an economic system whose methods are subject to regular change, and one which also increasingly confines the individual in large, disciplined organizations allocating to him specialized, narrow, recurrent tasks.[8]

"The population at large must be prepared to accept . . ." What a stirring vision this is for those who make the rules and direct the investments. The government official and the officer of the corporation are neither simply doing their jobs nor making their personal careers; they are engaged in a truly historic mission.

In the case of the Ciudad Guayana, the enterprise could draw on a particular set of ideas in the field of planning, around the concept of growth poles.

The Guayana project came into existence at just the time that U.S. planning professionals were coming to take a strong interest in regional planning.

> The spatial dimension of development was not an important
> theme for neoclassical economists, nor were regional differences in the outcomes of development popular topics among politicians in the emerging nations, bent on national integration and political control. . . . It was not until around 1960

that the regional aspects of economic planning attracted significant attention. This came about largely in reaction to the
practical problems of project planning . . . and the political
need for some visible concern about geographically balanced
national growth.[9]

Much of this interest in "regional planning" centered around one
version or another of the idea of growth poles, which, originated
by the French economist Perroux as a nonspatial concept of leading sectors, became, in the hands of the regionalists, an argument
for concentrated investment in particular places within backward
regions. The economic linkages between these growth poles and
the centers of economic power would simultaneously serve to
advance the entire national growth process and to overcome disparities in welfare between center and periphery.[10]
 One of the major works in the emerging regional planning
field indeed emerged from the Guayana Project itself. John Friedmann's *Regional Development Policy: A Case Study of Venezuela*
provided an intellectual rationale for the major features of the
program: a set of capital-intensive projects planned from Caracas.
"Although regional programs are intended to meet the requirements of local development" and "regional policy creates conditions favorable to an increased participation of local people in the
planning process," national control and national objectives were,
in Friedmann's view, clearly dominant over local interests.[11] Duly
setting the analysis of the Guayana Project in Rostow's framework of "stages" and "takeoff," Friedmann's book sees regional
planning as "a direct outgrowth of the triad which has the nation
as its basic mark of reference"—i.e., "national independence, national economic development, and national planning."[12] Friedmann sees the Guayana program as the exemplar, par excellence,
of a successfully technocratic approach to decision making. "The
Guayana program had given a dramatic demonstration of the
usefulness of technical reasoning for mobilizing financial resources

on a large scale. . . . Emphasis was to be placed on systematic surveys, rational diagnosis, strategies for goal achievement, and programming of specific project investments."[13]

The American planning team brought with them also a set of ideas centered around comprehensive, rather than simply project, planning. The Joint Center contract, which brought in the American city planners, was organized by Lloyd Rodwin, a professor at the Massachusetts Institute of Technology, Department of City and Regional Planning. He saw the enterprise as an entrepreneurial coup, as an opportunity for professional development, and as social reform. The first two aspects are more or less self-evident, given the size of the contract and the freedom of its Joint Center directors to hire staff who might represent the state of the planning art; it is the social reform aspect that seems to require some amplification.

Rodwin had come to Venezuela at the first instance at the invitation of a former student—one of a group of smart young Latin American planners who, as students in Cambridge, had organized and asked Rodwin to chair a course on housing in developing countries. After the fall of the Pérez Jiménez dictatorship, the former student, still identified with the political left, entered the newly elected Betancourt government. In this position, he now invited Rodwin to Venezuela to consult on housing problems. While there, Rodwin was introduced to the head of the CVG; the conversation went on for three or four hours; eventually Colonel Ravard persuaded Rodwin to accompany a group of Americans—Adlai Stevenson among them—on a sightseeing trip to the Guayana. "I was captured by it. . . . There was a sense of frontier."

Rodwin's view of planning was largely shaped by Charles Abrams, a very lively and reformist planner, as well as by the housing reformer Catherine Bauer, and Rodwin had a very strong sense of the planner as reformer. "Ravard's point of view was very right of center," he told me in April 1983.

My friends were all left of center. My friends saw me as someone who might correct the General's point of view. . . .

There was a completely inadequate conception of how development should occur. They thought of it as physical planning—they didn't care about the other dimensions. Our main
concern was to introduce social and economic considerations
into planning.

I thought that if you could introduce solid technical thinking, it would be solid thinking socially.

He saw the project as "a chance to do integrated development."
He insisted to Colonel Ravard that the project must be multidisciplinary: "It should include a range of people with different skills
and perspectives." He insisted, over Ravard's objections, that the
American planners must have Venezuelan counterparts. He
"thought it should be set up to be an opportunity to learn—
therefore it needed a relationship with the university."

Social planning technique was to humanize the technocracy of
the project. Planning would tame and socialize economic growth.

For the urban designers and other city planners, the project
carried a unique weight of idealism. They wanted not simply
building and economic growth, but also a community. They
wanted not merely a city, but a beautiful and humane city.

In retrospect, it appears that the whole focus on city planning
was itself a modification of a program which was rooted elsewhere, in specific programs of investment. It *is* true that left to
themselves, the Venezuelans would have done some city planning.
Indeed, before the Americans came on the scene the planning staff
in the Ministry of Public Works had already made a city plan for
the area—rapidly conceived, formalistic in character, and appar-
ently, judging by the rapidity with which it was abandoned when
the Americans came on the scene, backed by minimal institutional
commitment.[14] But the center of the Venezuelans' thinking seems
to have been projects such as the dam and hydroelectric power

plant of Macagua, the steel mill, the new dock, roads, and the housing projects for technical personnel which were in the works. The engineers of the CVG—the Division of Urban Development—continued to push ahead with projects and to speak derisively of the *espiritistas* of the Planning Department. Their views closely reflected those of the local elites at the site. At the head of the agency, Colonel Ravard was intent on his particular grand project: the Guri Dam. At what point the new city itself became a central CVG goal is not now clear. The new city appears nowhere in the 1960 charter of the CVG.

According to the Organic Statute for the Development of the Guayana, the CVG was responsible for:

- Studying the resources of the Guayana, both in the area of development, as well as outside the area, when the nature of the resource makes this necessary.
- Studying, developing and organizing the exploitation of the hydro-electric potential of the Caroní River.
- Programming the integrated development of the Region in line with the priorities and framework of the Plan of the Nation.
- Promoting the industrial development of the Region, through both the public and private sectors.
- Coordinating the activities in the economic and social field carried out by the various public agencies in the region.
- Contributing to the organization, programming, development and operation of those public services necessary for the development of the area.
- Carrying out any other task delegated by the National Government, including operations outside the area when there is a close linkage to the development program of the area.[15]

The program is one of resource development projects, plus "those public services necessary for the development of the area."

It seems to have been largely the American consultants who converted this mandate into planning a new city.

In part, the city planning enterprise represented infrastructure
for projects: "those public services necessary for the development
of the area." In part, like the earlier Ministry of Public Works
plan it had superseded, it was intended to attract investment and
dramatize a governmental commitment to the development of
the area.

> Having decided to foster the growth of an industrial city in the
> Guayana, the Venezuelan government and the Corporación
> Venezolana de Guayana (CVG) were faced with the difficulties
> of attracting investors and elite residents to the area. The Guay-
> ana had neither the physical nor the social nor the cultural
> climate that appeal to the Venezuelan elite. Creation of a high-
> quality physical environment was one way of coping with
> these problems. Urban design could be counted on to dra-
> matize the nation's commitment by producing strong and clear
> images of a future great city, and to create images of an at-
> tractive city—comfortable, efficient, and urbane. [16]

To summarize: The city was in some sense necessary as social
infrastructure: it comprised the housing and social services for the
workers, the transportation necessary to move people and goods.
To translate the requirement for infrastructure into one for a "high
quality physical environment" was justified by another argument
stemming from the primacy of development projects; it would
attract the investment and the technically and managerially skilled
persons that the projects required. It would do this in two ways:
by constituting an environment where such elites would want to
live and set up shop, and by demonstrating a government commitment to the whole development enterprise.

But the behavior of the city planners during the course of the
project shows that there was something more to it than that.

There has always been a Utopian strain in the urban design profession. Through Ebenezer Howard's "garden cities" one can see the distant echoes of Owen's "cooperative village" and Fourier's society based on "passional attraction."[17] The planners of Ciudad Guayana thought of themselves as practical persons, anything but Utopian, and they would have energetically disavowed the suggestion that they might be environmental determinists. But the evidence is that there was something of both in their thinking. Rodwin's conception of the planning enterprise had relied on comprehensive planning to humanize the projects of economic growth. The city planners called on urban design to create a humane world around the projects and to generate a sense of community in a setting of economic competition and class conflict.

Notes

1. CVG, Economic Division of the Planning Department, *Economic Program: Key to the Development of Venezuela* (Caracas: CVG, 1965), 4.

2. Louis Lefeber, "Some Observations on the Guayana Project" (CVG, División de Estudios, Planificación e Investigación [DEPI], Staff Working Paper B-74, Caracas, July 10, 1964), 13.

3. Marta Vallmitjana, interview with author, February 1, 1982. See also Alexander Ganz, "The World Bank Guri Mission: Comments on Meetings and Discussions Held; Recommendations" (Memorandum, Joint Center Guayana Project, July 27, 1962).

4. Frank Bonilla and José A. Silva Michelena, eds., *Studying the Venezuelan Polity: Explorations in Analysis and Synthesis* (Cambridge: MIT Center for International Studies, 1966), 495–96.

5. Hollis Chenery, *Redistribution with Growth: Policies to Improve Income Distribution in Developing Countries in the Context of Economic Growth; A Joint Study by the World Bank Development Research Center and the Institute of Development Studies, University of Sussex* (London: Oxford University Press, 1974).

6. Paul Streeten et al., *First Things First: Meeting Basic Human Needs*

in Developing Countries (Oxford: Oxford University Press, for the World Bank, 1981).

7. W. W. Rostow, *The Stages of Economic Growth: A Non-Communist Manifesto* (Cambridge: Cambridge University Press, 1965), 14.

8. Ibid., 20.

9. Clyde Weaver, "Development Theory and the Regional Question: A Critique of Spatial Planning and Its Detractors," in *Development from Above or Below: The Dialectics of Regional Planning in Developing Countries,* ed. W. B. Stohr and D. R. Fraser Taylor (New York: John Wiley and Sons, 1981), 74.

10. Ibid.

11. John Friedmann, *Regional Development Policy: A Case Study of Venezuela* (Cambridge: MIT Press, 1966), 18.

12. Ibid., 5.

13. Ibid., 160.

14. However, as María-Pilar García pointed out in a letter to me of June 11, 1985, this plan was more realistic than the expensively drawn plans which superseded it, in that "the distribution and location of the population (in relative figures) corresponded to those existing today."

15. CVG, Economic Division of the Planning Department, *Economic Program,* 11.

16. William Porter, "Changing Perspectives on Residential Area Design," in *Planning Urban Growth and Regional Development,* by Lloyd Rodwin et al. (Cambridge: MIT Press, 1969), 253.

17. Clyde Weaver, "The Precursors of Regional Planning: Utopians, Anarchists, and Geographers," in *Regional Development and the Local Community: Planning, Politics, and Social Context* (New York: John Wiley and Sons, 1984), 31–56. On the Utopian strain in city planning, see also: Robert Fishman, *Urban Utopias in the Twentieth Century: Ebenezer Howard, Frank Lloyd Wright, Le Corbusier* (New York: Basic Books, 1977); and Harold Orlans, *Utopia Ltd.: The Story of the English Town of Stevenage* (New Haven: Yale University Press, 1953), 79–121.

Chapter 3

First Stage: The Platonic City and the Aristotelian City

Getting Started

There were, of course, a number of practical problems in bringing the Joint Center Guayana Project into existence.

In the first place, the two directors of the Joint Center, Lloyd Rodwin and Martin Meyerson, had to convince their board to support the enterprise. This was not easy. One member of the board even resigned rather than support the proposal, feeling that this sort of planning work was properly the role of a private consultant. Other board members were apprehensive about working in Venezuela: Would there be too much instability and violence? Would Betancourt turn out to be a dictator or a communist? Some felt that the Joint Center should only work in Boston; others, that working in Boston was likely to lead to unhealthy political involvements.[1] Eventually the board supported a proposal for a program in which the Joint Center would provide consultants to the CVG in applied research, training, and planning, and simultaneously carry out a related program of scholarly research.

With the project well underway in 1963, the board members were flown to Venezuela to see their project at first hand. They visited the dam, the steel mill, and the anthropologist's mudwalled house, and listened to reports on the work. They expressed themselves as well satisfied.

But in the meantime, the negotiations between the Joint Center

41

and the CVG were followed by a bizarre episode. The contract
was signed in Cambridge, in English. Colonel Ravard said it
wouldn't be final until translated and signed in Spanish. He left
for Venezuela. Next day the contract was found in a Cambridge
trash can. Rodwin and Meyerson were disturbed and mystified.
Was everything off? They wanted to know, but were afraid to
ask. Three months later the Spanish version arrived—signed.[2]

Creation of the proposed interdisciplinary team proved more
difficult in execution than in conception. Finding staff who were
both appropriate and available was not easy. On May 5, 1961, a
letter from Martin Meyerson to the president of Harvard proposed the appointment of Norman Williams, Jr., an expert in
planning law, as the project director.[3] Williams did, indeed, go
to Venezuela to head the project. His tour of duty ended in December 1962, when long-standing disagreements came to a head
and he returned to the States. (This left the project, for most of
the initial contract period, without a director in residence.) Of the
two appointments proposed along with Williams, only one, that
of Wilhelm von Moltke as the director of urban design for the
project, was in fact accomplished. Von Moltke's major prior experience was in working with Edward Bacon in designing the
redevelopment of central Philadelphia; as a consequence, Bacon
was himself brought in briefly as a consultant to the Guayana
Project.

A great deal of effort and correspondence over the summer
and fall of 1961 was devoted to the search for a staff economist
and a staff sociologist. There was some resort to temporary economic consultants. In the fall of 1961 a "second man" in the field
of economics was engaged. In November Alexander Ganz was
hired to head up the economic analysis in the project. However
it was not until early 1962 that Ganz actually began work. On
October 25, Williams wrote:

After a couple of months' work, we have prepared a broad
layout for the city, and we are becoming increasingly confident

that most of the elements of this plan make very good sense. The major problem is that, since our economic staff is only beginning to arrive now, obviously much of the basic analysis has not been done; the urban design has been getting ahead of itself.[4]

The sociologist took even longer to find; when suitable persons were located they proved, in the end, unavailable. In the interim, discussions were held with a French group. On December 20, Norman Williams wrote of discussion with "M. Celestin of the Economie et Humanisme group" on how to develop leadership, how to "break the pattern of passively waiting for something to be done from above," and how to generate cottage industry, but adds that "we should continue our effort to obtain our sociologist, who would work with such a group."[5] On January 19, the MIT sociologist Daniel Lerner is asked to set down "the special qualification for a resident sociologist on this job," "the extent to which the resulting volume is likely to qualify as a sociological classic," and "the role and general content of a possible accompanying social action program."[6]

In the end, in February of 1962, I was rather hastily engaged as project anthropologist and went to Venezuela on two weeks notice amid some rather ribald speculations as to why anyone should claim that "they need an anthropologist right away." Fortunately for my peace of mind, nothing had been said of a "resulting volume . . . likely to qualify as a sociological classic."

While those responsible for the Joint Center project were still struggling to get their team in place, the underlying issue as to "projects" versus "city" surfaced in a dispute between the planning division and the management of the steel mill, also a part of the CVG, about housing for steel mill employees. The division managing the steel mill wanted to build housing just south of the plant. The planners argued costs of a new infrastructure and the loss of flexibility if the city failed to grow as predicted, in having a little subcity off at the west. The steel mill division argued

contractual obligations to the union and the cost of transport—
which, in Venezuela, is by law paid in large part by the firm.
There was a meeting at which the head of the CVG, Colonel
Ravard, sided with the steel mill. Eventually, the controversy was
resolved in favor of the planners and the unified city.[7] But the
issue was one which roused powerful feelings. On November 28,
1961, Norman Williams writes:

> This is a period of considerable tension and difficulties here;
> and we are watching and attempting to be as helpful as we
> can. The siderúrgica [steel mill] strike has apparently left major
> scars, including a near showdown between the planning group
> within the Corporación satellite town out by the plant. This
> showdown was postponed, but will come fairly shortly. Ap-
> parently the lack of housing was a major cause of the strike;
> and it is even being alleged that planning delays in getting this
> started may wreck the plant and even the whole Corpora-
> ción—which will give you the current mood.[8]

The issue as to the role of the city in the whole development
mandate of the CVG appeared to have been settled. But it was
to surface again later during the years of development after the
Joint Center Project had come to an end. Meanwhile, in the midst
of such substantive issues and the tensions of organizing an international team in a foreign setting, planning got underway.
What did planning a city mean?

Perspectives on the City

There are many ways to think of a city. A city can be thought
of as built form—buildings, open spaces, passages, barriers. It
can be thought of as a system of rules and regulations—taxes,
building codes, rules of ownership and tenancy. It can be thought
of as social relationships and social institutions—neighborhoods,

organizations, ethnic groupings. It can be thought of as an arena of power and of the political arrangements which organize power. It can appear as an economic system—capital investment, supplies of labor, housing and land markets. In reality, any city is all of these. Since each way of looking represents an aspect of a single reality, any one of these ways of looking must in the end lead to the others. Nevertheless, it makes a difference where one begins. Where the architect sees a skyscraper with a particular form, the developer, conscious of the rules under which building takes place, sees the zoning envelope; meanwhile, a community group that wanted another use for the land may see the building as a victory for intrusive capitalism. Each way of seeing represents the line of sight from a particular position in society; each way of seeing also proposes different criteria for what is important, and suggests different kinds of action with respect to the building.

There was a deliberate effort to include within the Guayana project team the widest variety of specializations. Since every professional specialization carries its own distinctive kind of viewpoint, there were a variety of perspectives on the city. There were urban designers and architects, economists, transportation planners, legal experts, a political scientist, an anthropologist. But the various perspectives did not enter equally into the planning process. Indeed, this would surely not have been possible. The Rashomon multiple vision supports speculation; but for action, we require a line of analysis, a more or less coherent conception of the problem to be addressed. The dominant perspective then organizes the others as contributions to acting on the problem which has been set as central.

The anthropologist, for example, was urged to contribute ideas on "customs and values" relevant to planning housing and commercial facilities, and on "social problems connected with" the development of the city, but not to raise questions as to whether the activities of development planning, taken as a whole, were socially beneficial.

In the Guayana project, the two main professional perspectives which dominated the enterprise were that of the urban designers and that of the economists. As will be seen, these two perspectives did not so much interact and fuse into a new or integrated perspective as divide the turf. They appeared as complementary; the economists described the economic base, and the designers designed around it. Each group of professionals continued to think in its own distinctive way and to use its own techniques for understanding the city and proposing for its future. In what follows there will be an attempt to show the nature of each professional perspective. What did they see as important? What did they take as data? How did they conceive of their own role? But it is also important to look at what the professionals tended to leave out. What were the questions that it seemed impossible to formulate?

In any case, one result of the delays in finding a complete interdisciplinary team was to put the urban designers in the position of identifying the issues and structuring a work program for the planning enterprise. When the economists got to work, the designers radically changed their conception of city size; when the anthropologist joined the staff, there were efforts—serious in intent, if not altogether successful in practice—to work out issues of the social implications of physical form. But the original conception of the Guayana project as interdisciplinary in its basic approach to issues, with decisions as to physical form emerging from a social and economic analysis of the function of the city, was never truly tested in practice.

Caracas versus "The Site"

An important constraint on the planning process derived from the choice that was made early on, and without much explicit deliberation, to base the planning operations four hundred miles away from the site of the city itself, on the thirteenth floor of the Shell Building in Caracas—"stuck to the air-conditioning" as people in Guayana derisively referred to the situation. In 1962, Norman Williams, the project director, reviewed the pros and cons in a letter:

> Finally, there is the major question of the location of the Corporación's principal offices, which we debate from time to time. The natural thing is to wonder why on earth they should be in Caracas instead of in the site; the TVA would not dream of being in Washington. My current judgement is as follows: for the present planning period, the principal offices should remain in Caracas, in contact—much more contact—with the main government departments concerned with planning the region. However, a schedule should be set up very soon for moving the Corporación's office to Ciudad Guayana, and a series of planned stages starting in a year or two. Moreover, the Corporación's staff on the site should be tripled or quadrupled, and the present extraordinary lack of communication between Caracas and the site must be broken by systematic liaison, and is really not all that difficult to arrange; as one detail, first class instantaneously communication equipment should be installed immediately (Orinoco Mining, right upstairs, can press a button and speak to their field officers instantly). We have often waited for hours to speak and sometimes for two weeks trying to get in touch with Mr. and Mrs. Peattie.
>
> The above recommendations, for staying on in Caracas for some time seem a bit on our side, but I think there are sound reasons for this. First, the federal structure of the Venezuelan government is 95% paper and 5% reality; everything of any importance is now run through Caracas. In these stages of planning a city, constant and immediate communication with other government agencies is imperative for certain planning operations. For example, our economic staff could not work without regular meetings with Cordiplan and the Banco Central; our work on standards and public facilities requires con-

stant communication with the Ministry of Education and others. Granted the Corporación's permanent staff does not do much of this, though they should. Second, the colonel undoubtedly feels that he must be in a position to be in continued contact with the President and I should hesitate to dispute his judgement on this kind of point (it may not be totally relevant in considering his over-all position in the country to note that, when high military conferences were called to decide how to deal with rebellions in Carupano and Puerto Cabello, he was called to both immediately and went). In the third place talking about moving everyone down immediately is pure rhetoric. It has taken us a year to design and get moving a project for a thousand houses desperately needed for the steel plant workers; it is practically impossible to get more than one half dozen houses in the whole future city at the present time. Moving one of two hundred people, many of them high level executives, to the site is not something that can be accomplished by the decision that simply someone wants to do it. Finally, such a decision will be resisted to the last stand by a large number of people involved, and needs time to be worked out. I have not the slightest doubt that many of the key personnel would leave the Corporación rather than move, and the Corporación cannot afford to dispense with their services now. [9]

The last comment was eventually proved justified when the CVG in 1974 finally transferred planning to its newly built headquarters in Guayana. A new staff had to be hired; those who had worked in Caracas remained there.

During the early planning years of the project, as it became clear that the CVG was not going to move, members of the American staff from time to time discussed sending part of the staff to live and work on site. The anthropologist, following professional tradition, bought a squatter shack by the Orinoco and lived in it. Another young architect and his wife did the same.

For a period, the Puerto Rican housing specialist and his wife lived in the CVG camp at the dam. But although several members of the engineering division took up residence on the site, as did social workers, even the steel mill was largely run from Caracas, and the planners related to the city for the most part via maps and plans, fleshed out with visits of a day or two at a time.

Part of this was surely the inconvenience of living in a frontier city, very short of middle-class standard housing and urban amenities. Norman Williams's family group included elderly members with special needs; he wrote that a swimming pool would be helpful. Wilhelm von Moltke's wife was a concert pianist and needed a first-class piano.

But one was really out of step with the team in living at the site. I had a distinct sense that moving into a squatter shanty beside the Orinoco had made me appear as something of a freak, and ruined whatever credibility I might have had. My husband felt exceedingly disconnected from the rest of the design team. A Venezuelan engineer, working twelve- and fourteen-hour days on projects of building, clearance, relocation, and negotiation with the local government was infuriated to be asked in the Caracas office, "And what do you find to do down there?"

From the perspective of the CVG, being in Caracas made every kind of sense. The CVG was one agency competing for power and resources among others and needed to keep its fences mended. The planning effort was a regionalization of national objectives; it was not focused on the people and institutions already on what the planners persisted in referring to as "the site." Since the CVG as an entity was to be in Caracas, the planning staff remained in Caracas.

This made a difference for the kind of planning that was done. Planning came to be that activity carried out with magic marker sketches on tracing paper, staff conferences, and statistical tables; it became possible to see the offices as the locus of action, and to ask an overworked and extremely engaged engineer at the site, "what do you find to do down there?" Indeed, as will be seen, there even came into use a terminology distinguishing activities on the site (called "fire fighting") from those activities in the Shell Building (called "planning").

The Urban Designers

Early in 1962 there was a meeting of the urban design team in Caracas. The topic was the general form of the city. Each staff member appeared with a sketch plan done in magic marker on a piece of tracing paper with which to illustrate his or her own analysis and proposal. Two members of the team, both, as it happened, naturalized Venezuelans of Catalan origins, had proposals which, while different one from the other, were like each other and different from those of the rest in starting from an analysis of the existing pattern of growth in the settlements already at the site. They were reproved by the head of the team for "abdicating the function of the designer." It was the role of the designer, they were told, to determine what the city's future form *should* be, not to describe what it was evolving into.

It is important to understand that the designers' tendency to marginalize or totally ignore the activities of the people and organized institutions actually at the site—even the practice of referring to a municipality with around fifty thousand people as "the site" as though it were tabula rasa—did not represent social irresponsibility and lack of caring, but rather the reverse. They did indeed care about the well-being of the people of the city, but in their own way, via their own professional perspective.

The project's chief designer summarized the goals of his enterprise:

> The design must be congruent with the terrain, the natural conditions, the forces acting upon it, and the functional organization of activities. It must fulfill the human needs of its

inhabitants and further social adjustment. It must accommodate change over the passage of time. It must offer interesting visual experiences. It must create order, a sense of unity, and a memorable image. It must emanate a sense of beauty that will foster pride in and loyalty to the city.[10]

Urban design is understood as mediating between the technical and the human, as fulfilling human needs—for "interesting visual experiences," "social adjustment," "sense of unity," and "pride in and loyalty to the city." But it does so by a particular kind of top-down professional activity called *design*.

The central focus of the project was, of course, economic growth through industrial development. But the designers came at this "materialistic" goal in what might be described as a very idealistic way. In developing strategies for economic growth in Ciudad Guayana, the designers placed a very large emphasis on urbanity and amenity. They did not think just of designing a city with suitable locations and infrastructure for industry; they envisaged a beautiful city, with agreeable neighborhoods and public spaces. In part this was because they saw urbanity and amenity as critically important means for attracting the technical elites and the outside investors who were thought to be crucial to the development process. In retrospect, the primacy of this "city beautiful" theme can be seen to have carried a great weight of social idealism for the designers. They saw it as important to develop a city about which people could feel positive and they saw design as an important tool for this end. They had a substantial commitment to building community, both at the neighborhood and at the citywide level, and their preoccupation with the city center, characterized as "the heart of the city," was both promotional or elite-attracting and an aspect of their commitment to community. Furthermore, they had a strong commitment to serving their clients—including, perhaps especially, their low-income ones—through the right kind of design. That was the reason for having an anthropologist on the project, and they often asked counsel on the "customs, needs, values" of the Venezuelans. They also commissioned a study—which unfortunately got completed far too late in the process to be utilized in the planning process—of the way in which the people of the site perceived the city.[11] These were, then, the very models of modern socially conscious designers.

The Economists

When the economists arrived to pick up their role in the project, they altered the ideas of the designers substantially, but not in such a way as to alter the sharp differentiation between "planning" for the "new city" and guiding the growth and development of the existing one. Indeed, the city of the economists was at least as discontinuous with the present as that of the designers and in some ways rather more so, for there was less "fire fighting" in their practice, and the planning theory in use, relying heavily on the magic of capital investment, did not dwell much on the evolution of institutions, technology, and human skills.

The economists saw the city as a frame for new investment in modern industry. Their written output depicted the rich natural resources of the region: the iron, the hydroelectric potential, the Orinoco shipping channel, and identified the industries which might be attracted to the area to constitute the "economic base" of the new city. On this base were calculated secondary industries and a need for labor; this, in turn, constituted the basis of population projections for the future. Their promotional optimism for the developmental possibilities of the area naturally produced rather expansive projections of population growth. A city which had been thought of as capable of accommodating 100,000 people in the first stage and 250,000 in the next twenty years was declared to be likely to grow to 415,000 by 1975 and by 1980 to top 600,000. The designers were shocked at how large a city Ciudad

Guayana was to be, and altered their plans accordingly. The economists' projections also showed them that major industries were bound to be in the western part of the city; the center of population would naturally also be to the west.

In retrospect, one sees that the economists were subject to the classic distortion of planning information; they were, above all, development promoters, charged with stimulating the investment that their projections showed to be potentially feasible and desirable. Since the same reports that made the projections on which planning was based were the documents shown to potential corporate investors in order to encourage them to invest in the region, there was a drift of optimism. As one of the economists said to me once, "If you don't believe it, it won't happen." In the outcome certain planned industrial clusters have failed to materialize and the city has not, in fact, grown as projected. (I usually refer to this as the Bay of Pigs syndrome, since a more dramatic and damaging instance of similar promotional optimism undercut the ill-fated invasion of Cuba.)

In any case, looking back, it is interesting to see what the economists' way of working did *not* change in the designers' outlook. The economists, even more than the designers, dealt in the future, a future even more discontinuous from the present, given the optimism as to size. Furthermore, the germ or embryo of that future was out there in corporate bodies like Reynolds Aluminum, not in the entrepreneurs of actuality. The economists had even less occasion than the designers to visit "the site."

The economists projected and promoted an industrial base for the future city and, tracing functional linkages between various industries, set their locations. The designers took these projections as the parameters with which urban design must deal.

With respect to the goals and values of planning, as with respect to subject matter, the economists divided the turf with the designers rather than confronting or modifying the ideas of the latter. The discussions and writings of the economists for the most part conspicuously lacked either the idealistic social goals of the designers or an alternative set. It would not have occurred to them to say, like von Moltke, that they must "fulfill the human needs" of the city's inhabitants and "further their social adjustment," much less "foster pride in and loyalty to the city." In general, the economists saw themselves as practical men in the pay of people who knew what they wanted and who had hired them to help them get it. The task at hand—development—was one that needed no particular justification or embellishment, since its importance was self-evident.

The projections as to the future economic development of the city were necessary to bring about capital investment in the present, and the capital investment in the present would bring about the state of things projected for the future. There were, among the economics staff, a couple of dissidents who would have liked to see the program cast into more idealistic terms. One of these men made an effort to withdraw from the project when he found on arrival that, as he put it to me, "they meant by development something like real estate development." He was particularly troubled by the promotional optimism as to the potential for certain industries and at the planners' lack of concern for creating jobs. Another dissident economist argued for a concern not only with job creation, but with food production in the region, also as a way of improving the condition of the working class. But the only agricultural projects of interest to CVG were high-technology capital-intensive schemes for export crops in the Orinoco Delta.

In general the economists were not particularly impressed by agricultural, employment, and income concerns among certain staff. The "self-evident" utility of economic growth freed them from moral doubt, and their experience in government consulting had given them a healthy respect for political reality. Thus they were capable of a mood of cheerful cynicism quite foreign to the designers. On one occasion, for example, they were required by the CVG to justify the heavy investment in urban infrastructure that had been projected in the plan. The chief economist came out of the meeting grinning, "I have just proved that street lights are the most productive investment you can make."

The Transportation Planners

In 1963 another special team of planning consultants was brought into the project. These were transportation planners who, armed with an early and still very exciting computer model, gave their account of the future distribution of population. The computer technology was altogether impressive to the Guayana staff, but the underlying conceptualization was simple enough; given the future location of industrial jobs, people would tend to minimize their distance from economic opportunity. Clearly, most people would live in the west. (Even less than the projections of the economists were these projections borne out by future events. The computer model had, unfortunately, failed to take account of some critical social facts. Industries pay travel time; and still more importantly, the CVG would never permit the raggle-taggle of working-class housing to be near the urbanizations for the well-to-do which held the terrain on the west. At present three-quarters of the city's population is on the east side of the Caroní.)

There was a certain potential for conflict between the transportation planners and the designers over the issue of goals. The transportation planners took a technical view of the problem; roads should connect various centers of activity in the most efficient way possible. The designers, on the other hand, perceived highways as of central importance in the esthetic experience of the city, as setting the form, and as providing views of the natural environment, especially the rivers. Both views, in the end, had something to do with the outcome. But the continuing presence of the designers and their general dominance over the planning process gave them substantial influence in this area too.[12]

The Platonic City and the Aristotelian City

Urban designers, economists, and planners all shared a perspective in which the city was to be the outcome of the design and planning going on in Caracas—not of the processes of investment, settlement, and political influence going on in the city of the present. Since I, as an anthropologist, saw the city from the latter perspective, someone once contrasted the two: "Willo [the chief designer] lives in the Platonic City; Lisa lives in the Aristotelian City."

The Aristotelian City appeared as businesses and neighborhoods and as people with individual and collective purposes. Among these were, for example, a man wanting to start a gasoline station and unable to get clearance from the planners as to where he might locate it; the municipal councilors, dealing with requests from constituents for a local school, for an extension of the water line, for street repairs; the Rotary Club, lobbying for local investment and deeply resenting the fact that the Pepsi-Cola bottling plant, unable to make any arrangement with the CVG planners, had gone south to Upata.

To be living on the site was to be in the midst of furious activity. It was a world of boosters, hustlers, prospectors, promoters, entrepreneurs, and developers. In spite of the official ban on construction, new shacks went up every day. I noticed with amusement a commercial block under construction directly behind a "Construction Prohibited" sign. In the coffee shop on the plaza or at the Spanish Club across the way the local politicians and businessmen strategized about a new bridge, discussed setting up a municipal program of housing loans, and complained of the CVG's inaction.

All this boosterism and entrepreneurship was shaping the growth of the Aristotelian City. But the local inhabitants were no more likely than the planners to see these activities as the way in which the official or Platonic City would come into existence.

After a conversation about the latest projects—the new dock, the technical school, the main avenue—it was common for a local resident to ask: "And where are they going to build Ciudad Guayana?"

Certain CVG staff came down to Guayana to work; they too soon became part of the Aristotelian City. One of the engineers "bootlegged" to the municipality plans for a new cemetery which the planners were not ready to site quite yet, and others began an unsanctioned subdivision. CVG Public Relations was paying the salary of a local Guayana region enthusiast with an office on the plaza. The office seemed to have little to do with plans for the future, but to be a center of programs on Guayana history and of cultural events bringing together the local intellectual elite.

The CVG staff in charge of the new low-income subdivisions sponsored by the development agency were something of an exception in their failure to meld into the local order. The head of the group, a woman social worker, was a devout Catholic— "more Catholic than the pope" as people put it—with a zeal for moral reform and a disinclination to take advice. The politicians of the municipality disliked her, and the local padre was angling for her transfer. He had found occasion to go to her office to shout her down for refusing a "reception area" lot to a man on the grounds that he was living off the earnings of his wife and daughter as prostitutes. Those in the general area could clearly hear the padre yelling that it was none of her business and that, in any case, it was the fault of the CVG's freeze on construction that the man could find no work of his own.

But as time went on, the new CVG urbanizations with their controlling staff of social workers also seemed to be part of the Aristotelian City. It was as if there were two governments in the area, one piece of the city governed by the municipality, the other by the CVG social workers.

The Platonic City of the designers appeared on schematic diagrams of urban form, renderings showing elegantly slim pedestrians strolling in the shade, prose which suggested that the Caroní Bridge might evoke the Ponte Vecchio. A great deal of time was put into designing a project for some of the future middle class that could set a high design standard for future urbanizations to follow.

> The shaded pedestrian circulation system connects each house pleasantly with play areas, sitting areas, kindergarten, elementary school, sports area, swimming pool, shopping area, bus stops and the park system beyond the boundaries of the neighborhood. . . .
>
> . . . All buildings are oriented toward the wind and are designed in a tunnel-like fashion to maximize its effect. In order to insure thorough ventilation, all rooms are exposed to the outside on both sides of the building. . . .
>
> . . . Through the center of the area runs a small stream, which widens into pools at focal points. This brook will water the trees along its edge,—a refreshing sight for residents and visitors.[13]

But pilot projects for lower income migrants also appeared as representing high esthetic standards and humane values.

> Houses are grouped along a well shaded common open space, which will provide opportunity for bolas criollas [bowling], sitting and the play of small children. There will also be a shelter for laundry and for showers.
>
> In front of each house is to be a shaded parking space. Each lot is wide enough to accommodate a house with 4 bedrooms, with patio and garden. If fully developed, the house will extend across the entire width of the lot, forming with adjacent houses a group of row houses. In order to make the best use of each lot, the street front of the houses is to be erected on the prop-

erty line. Thus a sense of enclosure around the common open space will be achieved.

These clusters of houses are grouped around a common open space which in most cases has only one entrance, thus eliminating through traffic. In a few cases it has been necessary to serve up to 20 houses through one of these clusters. And all houses front on these "private" open spaces.

It is believed that this layout will assist in fostering social structure and community spirit.

Shade is of the utmost importance, and the entire area is to be planted densely with trees.[14]

Thought was put into plans for modern roads and public services, plazas, and civic art.

Process and Design

When von Moltke returned to the city in 1981, he was delighted to see that the cul-de-sac urbanizations had developed very nicely, quite as he had envisaged in the planning period. But because the development agency was dilatory in getting in the water and services on which the plan depended, it took a long time for this to be achieved: so long, in fact, that the cul-de-sac plan was abandoned as a failure after the first experimental project.

Illustrative of the utopian quality of the designers' thinking is the stress in the visions quoted above on trees and water provision. In fact, the implementation process has been strikingly slow and halting in providing water in low-income urbanizations— even, in some cases, in high-income ones—and the development process has never been very successful in the planting of trees. One can see from the prose that during the early phase, which a colleague has called "alabaster city" designing, the possibility of such problems never really entered the designers' minds.

This failure to consider issues of implementation and the processes and institutions which would be required to create the city of the designers' vision was rather characteristic of the designers' way of working on the whole. It was, indeed, an aspect of the social idealism that these professionals valued in themselves. It was also supported by the tradition of expression via two-dimensional drawings, lacking the dimension of time or the representation of process through time. And, of course, it was made possible by physical separation from the site.

The outlook of the urban designers was rooted in the tradition of architecture, in which a designer or a group of designers— professional, middle-class—specifies the form to be produced by contractors and workmen. The contractors and workmen are thought of as entering the process for individualistic and commercial motives; it is the architect's function (at least, as the architect sees it) to represent higher esthetic and social values. This tradition helped to form some rather important implicit assumptions among the designers in the Guayana projects: first, that planning is quite different from implementation; second, that to get involved with the events and interests of the developing city of the present was to become mired in a lot of particularistic and rather ignoble concerns; third, that by focusing on the specifications for a desirable future city, urban designers were maximizing their potential for bringing about a socially desirable outcome. It was the *design,* as executed, not the process by which it would come into existence, that was to bring about the socially desirable outcome. In taking this view, the planners were of course bound to conflict with the people of the city, for whom issues of how long it was going to take and who benefited from the development process were bound to be critical.

The professional tradition that the designers brought with them into this situation included not only an art of designing the future city but also a vision of the future city as well. It would be a city of sweeping avenues, orderly public places, urban amenities for the well-to-do, and orderly settlements for the poor. This was a vision derived from a tradition of design for wealthy individual patrons and well-endowed public clients. The presence of this implicit vision of the future made it possible for the designers to think of the future as in a very real sense disjunctive with the present, as well as a clear improvement on it.

At one point during the project I had a conversation with one of the directors of the Joint Center about the tendency of the development agency to override the desires of people already living in Ciudad Guayana. He thought I was taking it too hard. After all, he pointed out, the current population was a small group of people compared to the population of the city of the future. I should have said that dealing with the people of the present was practice and institution-building for dealing with the people of the future, but I didn't think of it.

In any case, just as the designers conceived of the city of the future as a new city discontinuous with the development already on the site, they thought of the people who would live in it as different people. Colonel Ravard frankly said that Venezuela needed to import skilled people in order to develop, and in the city the focus on attracting corporate investors went with a focus on attracting managers and technicians, which entailed a model of change involving colonization by people different from those already there. Even when a social survey showed that much of the growth of population on the site was not migration but natural growth from the existing population and that those migrating in were in no substantial way different from those already there,[15] the mental set of the designers continued to be toward those different people who would somehow appear to inhabit those different forms they were creating.

The architectural model led the designers to think of designer initiative as central to the form of the future. They tended to ignore or underplay the other possible and actual sources of initiative in the situation. Isolated physically from the real city of the present and isolated organizationally and conceptually from the political and economic interest groups in which their enterprise had its being, they tended to leave these out of their calculations and to develop their own lines of work in relative isolation from other groups having interests in the situation.

The focus on design, as has been noted, emerged from the intellectual tradition of professional architecture. But it fitted nicely with the context in which these designers were working. The CVG was a national body, based in Caracas. It was established to further national goals. It did not wish to go in for working with or through local government—indeed, local interests were all too likely to get in the way of its purposes. Colonel Ravard believed—and said—that the less anyone on the site knew of the plans until they were all complete the better. Indeed, he once remarked at a meeting that he wished he could put everyone in the city under anesthetic until the city was finished. In the meantime, the designs for the city figured splendidly in the promotional brochures of the CVG. The people on the site—who did not think of it as the site of a future city but as a growing city of which they were citizens—were not, of course, under anesthetic and could not be wholly ignored. Indeed, more and more of them kept moving in. There were never any reliable statistics, but estimates were something like a thousand people a month. Meanwhile, construction was—in theory—frozen, to give the designers time to work out a design.

On May 1, 1962, the two members of the Joint Center staff living at the city site wrote:

> In our preliminary investigations of the social and planning problems of the site, we have met a remarkable difficulty: the problem which so far emerges most clearly seems to emanate from Caracas. This problem is the almost total paralysis of building and of urban development as a result of the CVG's control. . . .

. . . There now exist almost no places where people may legally build—either businesses or homes. The Banco Obrero still has some house sites left—all very small ones—but it will soon run out of even these.

Areas for professional housing are almost completely tied up.

We are told that the cemetery is full, and that no new cemetery can be built until plans for the city are developed.

Badly needed light industry on the San Félix side has no place where it can locate. The municipality has already disputed with the CVG over which of these two bodies might legally allocate industrial land.[16]

The activities in which the designers dealt with immediately pressing issues ("fire fighting") were sharply differentiated from planning and indeed were thought of as a distraction from planning. There was redesign of the Caroní Bridge so it could accommodate pedestrians. There was finding a different site for the aluminum plant from that already selected by the CVG. There was the development of "reception areas"—serviced building lots—to accommodate some of the lower-income population, and the siting of the new cemetery. In looking at the list, one is struck in retrospect by two things: first, that many of the "fires" were in fact struck by the engineers of the CVG (the bridge, the aluminum plant) and second, that response to people's immediate needs was at a level so minimal as to appear almost grudging. The reception areas were small, and to get a building lot in one required days of negotiation to prove that one was among the most deserving of the myriad claimants for the few lots. After siting a new cemetery, the Caracas group decided that perhaps, after all, they ought not decide so soon, and tried to take the decision back; an engineer based at the site took the local priest over and got him to bless the ground to prevent the decision being un-made.

Issues in the Urban Design Process

Particularly important during the first period of planning was planning for the city Center. Given the way in which the Caroní River divided the city into two socially distinct segments, the designers thought at first about developing the area in a "twin cities" format. But "because a strong urban image was needed to help overcome the sense of isolation in this frontier area, the idea did not survive for long."[17] Once it was determined that planning should be for a single unified city, the Center appeared to have a number of critically important functions. It would epitomize the *urban* atmosphere which was to be created. "To attract the type of people who are essential . . . an urban atmosphere is needed. This atmosphere is epitomized by the Centro." Furthermore, it would advertise the city nationally. "The early and dramatic development of the Centro would be a way of turning Venezuela's eyes to the interior."[18] Finally, it would build community.

Referring to the sharp visual contrast between the predominantly working-class city on the east of the Caroní and the higher-income settlements on the west, a memorandum of 1962 says: "I understand that there is at present a divisive sense of 'we' and 'they' on either side of the Caroní. The early development of a Centro for Santo Tomé would be a strong unifying force and would help give a sense of direction to the local population."[19] The organizing issue, during this period, was locating the Center. Consideration was given to three different locations on the San Félix side of the river. Then, considering the development of industry to the west, the Center was moved (in the designers' minds and on their plans) across the river. When the Joint Center board was brought to the site, the planners had to make and present a decision; in their presentation to the visitors they gave an account of the physical drama of a Center near the falls of the Caroní. But even as they were making their presentation, they were having second thoughts and concluding that the site by the river did not offer enough space for a Center; the Center must be on the ridge somewhat to the west.

Other issues concerning the Center seem, at this period, to have been treated as secondary to that of location. The first of these, which did at any rate receive a good deal of discussion, was the issue of what functions would be located in the Center. What should the city's heart consist of? In general, these functions were thought of as ceremonial (a plaza or open space of some sort), government/managerial (the CVG and local government buildings), and first-class commercial (preliminary drawings were made of a commercial center, for which Sears Roebuck and CADA (a Rockefeller-owned retail enterprise) were envisaged as prime tenants.

An issue which was only brought forward secondarily was that of implementation: How would the Center come into existence? Here the alabaster city mode of thought offered very little guidance. The CVG would, of course, build its own building and perhaps one for the local government, and it could execute a plaza. But much of the center was to be the outcome of investment by various private commercial interests. How would it be mobilized?

By 1965, when a few Joint Center staff were working on plans for the Center up in Cambridge, these issues had been confronted, and a strategy for dealing with them was proposed. But as will be seen in a subsequent account, the CVG's way of working rendered it unable to bring off the strategy. It could build its own building, not orchestrate other investors. The Center, as envisioned by the designers, never happened. There is at present no unifying center in Ciudad Guayana.

As the designers moved to execution, they began to understand the limitations of their power to implement. No contractor wanted to build the housing project which they had so painstakingly designed as a model of practice. It seemed to any contractor far simpler and at least equally profitable to follow a more conventional form. By the time the CVG itself built the project, planning practice was moving toward a model which we might call the subcontracted city: a form in which the designers would set design parameters and locations and permit development to take place in accordance with what other actors—private developers—were prepared to build.

One consequence of this way of working was an intensification of processes of class segregation, which the Americans saw as undesirable even as they found themselves collaborating in it. In the Aristotelian City of fifty thousand which was there when the planners entered the scene, there was a great deal of income and class diversity within the various neighborhoods—not because class prejudices were lacking, but because in the absence of a formally organized urbanization process there was no way to exercise them. There were no bounded "good neighborhoods," and people built where they could. For example, in the squatter settlement of El Roble, among the little cement-block houses of the working class and shanties of the very poor were a number of much more pretentious dwellings with masonry walls and wrought-iron windows and door screens belonging to doctors and other professionals.

The designers held many discussions as to the degree to which it would be possible to design for some degree of economic class mixture in the city, treating the issue as one of social prejudice, but here the Aristotelian City as well as the planning process itself got in their way. Straining toward diversity conflicted with what, to the CVG, was a more important set of goals: the attraction of investors and technical elites and the production of a city which would have the look of modern developmental success. Both these issues meant that the CVG would try to keep low-income neighborhoods away from the "good side" of the city. But in addition, there were the developers, to whom only a "package" of more or less identical dwelling units in one area was an attractive proposition. Thus new planned neighborhoods, each for a particular narrow income class, came into existence, and as they did, the better-established tended to leave the existing mixed neighborhoods and move into the new urbanizations, rendering the old neighborhoods more homogeneously lower-class than before.

Toward the end of the planning period, some of the designers became interested in the idea of a kind of planning which we might call that of the developmental city—upgrading the existing Aristotelian City via small units of new housing on vacant land and the introduction of collective services. A plan along these lines was developed for the squatter settlement called Dalla Costa on the eastern side of the Caroní River. But implementation seemed impossible. The CVG was not particularly interested, and no private developer could be found who would undertake the complicated task of doing these little units of building on diverse and spatially separated parcels of land.

Consequences

The tendency of the urban designers to focus on design rather than process and to think of the final outcome (the planned city) as discontinuous from the present caused them a good deal of trouble with respect to the implementation of their plans. Some of these have already been noted: the project for a pilot high-standard urbanization foundered on the failure to find a contractor willing to build it, and insufficient attention to the dynamics of timing meant that they were unable to get Sears Roebuck to tenant their Center.

But it went further than this. Not only did the designers have trouble in controlling the private actors in the city, they also had trouble controlling the CVG's own engineers. Because of the nature of their work, the engineers, whose central focus was, after all, building, were more consistently based "on site" and consequently developed social ties to, and a common outlook with, the local commercial-political elite. The engineers became extremely impatient with what they called the *espiritistas* of planning. At one point, as a sort of show of power, the engineers proceeded to lay out an urbanization on the eastern part of the city without so much as informing the planners. When planners came from Caracas, the local staff took the plan for the urbanization off the office wall to conceal the project. The head of the engineering division told me proudly: "The planners like to talk about a sequence: planning, design, implementation. Well, we've reversed it."

The architectural way of thinking, with its focus on final form and a high standard of amenity, allowed the designers to neglect the mundane issues of housing supply and to underestimate the reluctance within the CVG toward taking seriously the problems of housing for lower-income people. Some of the architects put in a great deal of thoughtful work in trying to improve the design of housing for the poor. When it became clear that public policy was not going to subsidize the poor to buy or rent architect-designed housing, but would make it possible for the poor to house themselves by the step-at-a-time upgrading process planners call "self-help," the architects of the Guayana Project still worked on model house plans which would improve the level of design. But the issues were not really design issues: they were issues of access to resources, especially land, and solutions to these, given the prejudices of the CVG, were not readily forthcoming.

Social and political forces—in particular, the extreme reluctance of the CVG to allow the progressive-development housing of the poor near the elite urbanizations—pushed residential growth to the east of the city instead of the west as was projected. The new contract-built neighborhoods to the west where the middle classes live are now counterbalanced by a vast area of shantytown step-at-a-time development housing to the east. The avenues and monuments of the alabaster city now lie in the midst of emerging forms and forces to which they bear only a minimal relationship. It is at least arguable that if the designers had conceived their role as a catalytic, mobilizing one in which they were only one of several forces and actors and had conceived the future as emerging from the present, they would actually have come a good deal closer to their goal of shaping the city of the future.

Finally, the architectural model of thought led the designers to misconceive the nature of the social issues in their work. They thought of their work as creation. It was that, but it was also allocation or distribution, and although the distributional issues were terribly salient they were very largely overlooked by the designers. This point could be made at almost every level of design.

In worrying about improving the standard of design in self-help housing the designers were focusing their social idealism in a way that took their attention away from the pressing issues of who would get access to more desirable urban locations.

When the designers made plans for a middle-income residential area they thought of the problem as ascertaining the design needs of a particular sort of clientele and creating an environment which would serve those needs. But in the process, they were allocating public resources to a particular social group—a point which was not lost on spokesmen for the poor in the developing city when they saw the new residential areas for the middle class rising near the business center on the steel mill side of the Caroní.

Interesting issues arose when the designers made plans for the new city Center on the ridge at the western end of the existing city. Here, as already mentioned, would be the central headquarters of the planning agency and a modern shopping center with Sears Roebuck as the prime tenant. A new avenue from the just-completed bridge across the Caroní would bring traffic straight into the new Center, bypassing the existing commercial district with its disorderly clutter of auto parts stores, dress shops, and

bars. The designers saw this work as creation. The local businessmen with interests in the existing commercial area saw it as
distribution; they saw that their customers were to be carried
away from them. They demanded a road connection to the new
avenue. Several of the designers expressed great indignation at
this pushing of special interests against the plan; they said the
businessmen were only thinking of their own pocketbooks. But
they did not apply the same analysis to Sears. They thought of
the plan as representing the general welfare, of which Sears was
somehow the instrument.

The architectural model of design carries within it an allocation
issue in the monopoly of information at the top. In a developing
city advance information is in itself a critical economic resource.
Where will the industries locate? How will the roads run? Where
will the customers be? For people in the growing city, the existence of a planning process brought not a higher degree of pre-
dictability but the reverse. It meant that at any time large and
unforseeable forces were likely to impinge on their environment
and shape their life chances. Those developers and industrial interests that the CVG wanted to interest in investing in the area
had access to this information; local people did not.

In summary, then, the designers were not only creating, they
were allocating. And they were allocating resources in a manner
that contributed to inequality within the city. They were not, of
course, the primary source of inequality; that lay in the nature of
the development process itself, which at least in the short run was
bound to increase inequality even while it boosted the GNP and
raised, we hope, the absolute level of living of the people at the
bottom. The project certainly brought up the level, absolutely
and relatively, of one of the poorest regions of Venezuela. But
while the designers did not intend to promote inequality in the
city, they were promoting a process which had inequality as one
of its characteristics, and their way of working in itself contributed to inequality.

This leads me now to a last comment on the social functions of the design process, one somewhat harder to document than the preceding but one that I see nevertheless as true and important. This is the function of making more generally acceptable a development process which had as one of its characteristics growing inequality.

Organizing their sense of social purpose around amenity and user needs at the individual level and around community at the social level provided the designers with no convenient grasp of issues of material interest and social conflict. At the individual level, interests appeared as preferences: they were referred to the anthropologist for advice on "customs and values." On the wider scale, issues of class and interest-group conflict were thought of as problems of building a sense of community and the orientation of newcomers. Thus it was possible for the designers to combine a very strong sense of social idealism with activities that contributed to unequal distribution of social advantage without ever being clearly aware of the fact that this was going on.

But this process was not simply one that shaped the vision of the designers themselves. It was also one that made it possible for the designers to project for others a kind of utopian vision of the future. In this vision, the activities of the CVG and their American consultants were transmuted from a set of profit-making projects from which specific groups benefited in various specific ways to a general development process for the benefit of the community as a whole. The "New City" was the material symbol of progress. The design approach to city building became the vehicle by which the social idealism of the designers could cast over the whole planning enterprise the rosy glow of the ideology of progress via economic growth.

Notes

1. Lloyd Rodwin, interview with author, April 5, 1983.
2. Ibid.

3. Martin Meyerson, letter to President Nathan Pusey, May 5, 1961.

4. Norman Williams, letter to Robert B. Mitchell, October 25, 1961.

5. Norman Williams, memorandum to Ganz, Martocci, and von Moltke, December 20, 1961.

6. Norman Williams, memorandum to Daniel Lerner, January 19, 1962.

7. Lloyd Rodwin, interview with author, June 2, 1983.

8. Norman Williams, letter to Lloyd Rodwin and Martin Myerson, Caracas, November 28, 1961.

9. Norman Williams, letter to Robert B. Mitchell, July 12, 1962.

10. Wilhelm von Moltke, "Urban Design Intent: Three Case Studies" (Manuscript, January 1983), 76.

11. Donald Appleyard, *Planning a Pluralist City: Conflicting Realities in Ciudad Guayana* (Cambridge: MIT Press, 1976).

12. For a more extended account of the interaction between transportation planners and designers see Penfold, "Urban Transportation," 178–201.

13. Wilhelm von Moltke, "Design Criteria for Area No. 4 Puerto Ordaz" (Memorandum to Norman Williams, Jr., March 1962), 2.

14. Wilhelm von Moltke, "Ideas Underlying the Design of El Roble" (Memorandum, Caracas, April 19, 1962), 2.

15. J. S. MacDonald, "Summary Recommendations, Migration and Population Policy for Guayana" (Joint Center for Urban Studies, University of the West Indies, Trinidad and Tobago, n.d., Mimeographed); see also J. S. MacDonald, "Migration and Population of Ciudad Guayana," in *Planning Urban Growth and Regional Development,* by Lloyd Rodwin et al. (Cambridge: MIT Press, 1969), 109–25.

16. Roderick and Lisa Peattie, memorandum to Norman Williams and Willo von Moltke, May 1, 1962.

17. Von Moltke, "Urban Design Intent," 58.

18. William Alonso, "Development Alternatives for the Urban Mass and the Centro of Santo Tomé" (CVG, file no. A-6a, September 25, 1962, Mimeographed), 9.

19. Ibid.

Chapter 4

Planning Gives Way to Development

The departure of the Joint Center team in 1964 did not mean that planning for the city was finished. That was never the planners' idea. The process envisaged was one of successive revisions that would permit a gradual refining of the program and of the original solutions. There was still a staff in urban design, among these a couple of the Americans staying on. Nor did the Joint Center withdraw from the project overnight; during 1965, up in Cambridge, members of the Joint Center team were doing detailed work on the design and programming of the proposed Center on the ridge.

But the end of the Joint Center project did mark the end of one stage: a stage in which the idea of a planned city was given high visibility via a large, well-funded, international, multidisciplinary team. There had been urban development going on during the planning phase, but it was subordinated to planning by thinking of it as "fire fighting" and resisting it via the freeze on construction; there was planning going on during the next decades, but now planning was very much subordinated to development.

However, the period between the Joint Center planning project and the present divides roughly in the middle. The first decade is one of somewhat patchy implementation—a process of execution limited by the difficulties of attracting all of the private investments proposed, along with the limited capacity of the CVG to substitute for private investment. Some parts of the plan got built; some parts remained unrealized. The all-important commitment of the aluminum companies came to pass, but not the-metals and machinery complex. The city grew, but not as fast as had been predicted. The second decade was dominated, in contrast, by a glut of resources; the rise in oil prices suddenly multiplied several times over the funds available for Guayana. Now the problems of the city were reversed; the city and the needs of its inhabitants were swamped by the oil-boom-powered investment in heavy industry.

An important element of the city which got built by the CVG engineers in the early years was the great spinal avenue—Avenida Guayana—which was to link up the scattered settlements from the old town of San Félix on the east to the steel mill on the west. The bridge was completed, and a new port on the east of the Caroní. The development agency also planned and contracted a number of new residential areas. In an effort to bring population westward, nearer the center of industry and the Center, two major urbanizations were created south of Avenida Guayana on the west side of the Caroní. There were a number of institutional building projects: a technical training center, a church, some schools, a new hospital.

However, now that the project was less centered on planning and more on implementation, certain inherent problems of the design-grounded planning process with its institutional separation from ongoing processes at the site became apparent.

One of the urban development problems of the early period was the implementation of the Center, the location of which had so much preoccupied the urban designers in the early days. It had been thought of, with some passion, as "the Heart of the City"; it had been conceived as having important functions, both practical and symbolic, in providing a highly visible concentration of modern urban amenities. Finally, it had been argued that "the Center, with its potentially tremendous concentration of values in land and buildings," provided an opportunity for making the city at least in part self-financing; the "revenues gained from it can benefit the entire community and the development corporation."[1]

Now that it had finally been decided that the Center should be on the Alta Vista ridge west of the Caroní, there were issues of implementation. The dominant issue was how to get the Center off to a sufficiently concentrated and conspicuous start, given the relatively small total amount of commerce available for centering in a city still under 150,000 people. This problem was, of course, exacerbated by the desire to have the Center marked by modern, high-class commercial development. Much of the commerce that *was* springing up was anything but upscale—disorderly drygoods stores, hardware shops with hanging buckets and tools, cheap restaurants, neighborhood groceries. Furthermore, a small but growing center for prestige commerce had already become established next to the Orinoco Mining Company community in Puerto Ordaz.

One response to the issue was to try to get as anchor at least one large and high-prestige tenant. The choice from the beginning was Sears Roebuck, which had a large, upscale department store in the capital and which certainly had the intention of establishing a presence in Ciudad Guayana. It was to be joined by a Rockefeller chain. Negotiations with Sears for the starring role in the Center seemed at one point well advanced, but they fell through. One interpretation I have heard is that the planners took so long to decide on the location of the Center that Sears had found another spot; another story told is that Sears had already agreed when the Joint Center, seeing a closed process as improper, pressed for open bidding, thus delaying the decision too long.[2] In any case, by the time the CVG began developing its Center on the ridge, Sears had already constructed a six-story building down in the existing prestige shopping area of Puerto Ordaz.

A 1964 study on the economic feasability of the Center, still assuming that Sears and CADA would be its major tenants, concluded that "if uncontrolled expansion of competing commercial areas in Puerto Ordaz takes place before the Centro . . . is completed . . . this would cause the project to be financially unsound" and urged "direct and indirect controls on competing commercial growth elsewhere in Ciudad Guayana."[3] A second strategy proposed by a U.S. consultant was one which would accommodate the rather mixed bag of existing commercial offerings around the proposed Center but at a little distance; the "outside-in" strategy would lead to a gradual buildup of density and value of development.

When the Joint Center staff back in Cambridge in 1965 worked on preliminary designs for the Center they followed a line of thought somewhat along the lines of the outside-in strategy. Less prestigious commerce would play a role at the early stages and would be gradually phased out as the city grew and collected larger numbers of affluent shoppers. In the meantime, a physical design based on large "superblocks" with interior circulation was proposed as a way of reducing the visibility of the inferior commerce.

In the end, none of this worked out. Sears built in Puerto Ordaz. When the Center was not picked up by any large modern enterprise capable of putting a single development package in place, the CVG seems to have had neither the will nor the organizing capacity to orchestrate a bunch of small businesses as temporary placeholders.

The CVG did build in the Center its own new office building, a dramatic modern brick structure. But the municipal government declined to move to the adjacent parcel programmed for its use; the councilors saw the prospect of a new building as insufficient compensation for moving away from the body of voters and under the competing power of the CVG. Indeed, groups of citizens twice protested against the proposal to move municipal government across the river.[4] Administrative power in Ciudad Guayana is now located in two distinct centers on opposite sides of the Caroní. In the contrast between the grandeur of the CVG's

building and the modest buildings of the local government next
to the plaza of San Félix—even redecorated and air-conditioned
as they have been since my day—conflicts of power and disparities
of class position are manifest in physical form.

As for the idea of the Center as a source of income to offset
other development costs, this would, it became clear, run directly
counter to a deep-seated prejudice in the agency against acting as
a commercial landlord. Despite urgent advice from the American
consultants during the planning period,[5] the CVG eventually determined to sell the commercial land outright.

When I visited the city in 1971 the ridge designated for the
Center was occupied only by the CVG's own new office building.
Around this stretched blocks of red earth, marked by cement
curbings and street lights. Eventually, implicitly conceding defeat
on the original plan, the CVG sold much of the land to developers
who erected widely dispersed apartment towers in the area. The
Center, as conceived by the urban designers, never happened.

We might generalize the problems of implementation as follows. The CVG was not able, nor did it intend, to "build a city."
The idea was to construct some basic elements of the city, and
to encourage the private sector to do the rest; indeed, the stim-
ulation of private sector investment was one of the basic rationales
for the investment of government resources by the CVG. But the
CVG was so constructed, organizationally and ideologically, that
it could only deal with the private sector as it appeared in the
form of organized corporate entities: industrial corporations, real
estate development companies, Sears Roebuck. But the "private
sector" consisted in large part of an assemblage of tiny firms, like
the hardware and auto parts stores along the highway or the
families creating houses one by one with the aid of individual
contractors. The CVG had no way of dealing with such noncor-
porate actors and was not disposed to create one.

In theory, there could have been the invention of systems of
incentives and regulations that could have channeled this "private

sector" into the city-building process. Or, also in theory, the CVG might have found ways to work with intermediate institutions which were, in turn, in contact with the myriad of little local actors. But the CVG as a national institution was the vehicle of an idea of a modern and desirable city very much tied into a corporatized model of development and management, and the planners tended to see the ragtag existing private sector, and indeed even the municipal government that represented this private sector, as an encroachment on the site of the coming city rather than as the city in embryo.

The same underlying problems that afflicted the implementation of the Center afflicted implementation of another, and even more basic, concept in the plan. This was the distribution of population over the urban space. It will be remembered that when planning began, the majority of the (still rather small) urban population was living in or near the old town of San Félix on the east side of the Caroní; the steel mill, nearing completion, was eighteen miles away on the west side of the Caroní. The journey to work was not a trivial issue. Under Venezuelan labor law, companies had to pay travel time, so the price of the existing population distribution was paid not only in personal inconvenience but in the costs of production; every trip from San Félix to the steel plant was a tax on steel. The logic of industrial location meant that most of the new industries projected for the area would get located in the same sector of the city as the steel plant; the same logic of commuting cost would become magnified with time.

Everyone agreed that the distribution of population should reduce the journey to work, either by having more sources of employment on the San Félix side or having a higher proportion of the population living near the center of industry in the west. Planning proposed both. In any case, there was general agreement, "scientifically" supported by the computer models of the team of transportation specialists, that with time population would tend to shift toward the west.[6]

Those who reasoned from a "gravity model" of location that people would tend to live near jobs had, of course, to explain why it was not happening at the moment. The explanation in favor among the American planners was the Venezuelan labor law compensating workers for the journey to work; the view was that as Ciudad Guayana evolved into a "normal city" the regulation would be abrogated and normal gravity would exert its force.[7]

In fact, the chief reason that people were not living on the west side of the Caroní was that the CVG would not let them. On several occasions land invasions, often by workers of the steel mill, were repressed by police. As in the case of commerce, the agency wanted development—but only the right kind of development, and a kind which was quite beyond the means of most of the public. If the CVG, in its planning role, both predicted and hoped for a movement of the population westward, its prohibition of irregular building (shanties) to the west simultaneously made such a movement impossible for the majority.

As a member of the Cambridge group pointed out in his review of land development issues, the CVG had sharply conflicting objectives.

> On the one hand, all CVG officials were agreed that the west side should be dominant and should receive a preponderance of future growth. On the other hand, some top officials also wanted to keep all modern developments on the west side and relegate squatters' shacks and other aesthetically substandard structures to the older east side. Their goal was to build a thoroughly modern and attractive "new city" free from surrounding squatter villages—and therefore more attractive to potential executives and leaders than other Venezuelan cities already permeated with squatters.

However, the analysis showed that immigration of very
low-income households formed a large part of the total future
population growth. It would therefore be impossible to confine
the expansion of this group to the east side and still have a
preponderance of total growth occurring in the west side. This
posed a dilemma: should the CVG sacrifice the aesthetic and
social-class "purity" of west-side development in order to shift
most growth to that side, or should it sacrifice the size dominance of the east in order to maintain its "purity"?

Keeping "shacks" out of the west would also split the city
socially and politically. It would tend to create two groups that
were very distinct from each other socially and economically
as well as spatially—and therefore much more likely to split
into two separate legal entities as well. Since the city had only
recently been created by unifying these two areas anyway, such
a combined social-economic-spatial stratification would prevent it from ever really becoming a single city.[8]

The consultants' recommendation was to satisfy the demand
for purity by developing urbanizations each of which was ho-
mogeneous economically—but to have a mix of urbanization
types on both sides of the river. However, even this policy proved
difficult for the CVG to swallow, and the "shacks," which for
much of the working-class population constitute the first step of
housing development, were never accepted on the west.

In Venezuela, as in most of the developing world, a large part
of the population cannot afford to buy completed houses at U.S.
standards. Incomes are lower than those for whom this kind of
housing was invented; furthermore, the mortgage institutions
which would make possible long-term financing are not present.
So people build incrementally. A family acquires a plot of land,
sometimes by purchase, sometimes by squatting, puts up a pro-
visional shack with whatever comes to hand, and improves it
slowly over time.

The investment that in the U.S. system is rendered abstract—in the monthly mortgage payment—is here rendered visible in the shift from tin or earth to concrete block, from rough block to block plastered and painted, from one room to two, from two to three, from one story to two.

It was this process which the CVG was unwilling to permit on the "good side" of town, although it was going on in volume on the east side, even under CVG sponsorship in the so-called self-help projects. By 1973, the agency had come to accept the idea that shifting the population westward would require allowing lower-income families to live in the west, and was opening up a low-income urbanization nearer to industrial areas. Some of these projects would begin with a lower level of services in order to lower initial costs. But nowhere in the west was incremental building to be permitted; all the western projects involved housing constructed by the housing agencies, not by residents.

In effect, the CVG had in mind the development of the city by the private sector—but a different kind of private sector from that actually present. One may be reminded of Brecht's comment about the German government's announced dissatisfaction with the response of the German people to some measure it had announced: "They should get a new people."

It was difficult for the CVG to work with small, noncorporatized private actors; it was also not easy for it to work with other public bodies. Here institutional turf created problems from both sides. The CVG did not like to relinquish control; other national bodies, such as the Ministry of Education or Ministry of Public Works were not anxious to contribute to the project for which a rival agency, the CVG, already well-funded, would surely get the credit. Thus the planners' original concept that the CVG would gradually transfer more and more of the responsibility for the city to other public bodies and to private actors was difficult to achieve in practice. Some transfer of responsibility took place. In 1964 two semiautonomous bodies were set up: Fundación de la Vivienda del Caroní (FUNVICA) to do housing and Associación Guayanesa de Ahorro y Préstamo (AGAP), a savings and loan association. In 1966 the national agency took over the city's water and sewer system. But private investment relative to public has lagged compared to what the planners projected, and within the public bodies the CVG still dominates. Even up to the present the city continues very much as the CVG's responsibility, and it still gets blamed for the city's deficiencies.[9]

There is no record of public unhappiness over the failure of the Center to develop as planned. However, the deficiencies of the city as a place to live certainly did become a very live political issue. In 1971 there was an illegal strike of considerable bitterness at the steel mill; troops were called in and strike leaders arrested. The forces immediately precipitating the strike were, clearly, those of union politics—two unions on the left competing in radicalism. However, one of the demands which took six thousand workers out of the plant was for a company commissary that could compensate for the high prices of food in the city. "The situation, according to the workers, is aggravated since the enterprise has not been able to construct the houses necessary for the 6,000 workers, who must pay for transportation to get to their homes situated up to more than a hundred kilometers away."[10]

There were also complaints about the inequalities in the development of the city and specifically about the CVG's role in these inequalities. When I visited in 1971, people pointed out to me that the improvement of medical facilities in the city had actually worsened medical care for the poor: the new hospital was managed by the social security agency and thus served only insured workers; the old public clinic had been "given" to a private physician. Thus those who were neither regular employed workers nor self-employed professionals would have to go to the region's capital for care or go without.

The agency's role in building luxurious private schools had evidently generated substantial bitterness, for when the agency

gave a new laboratory to the Catholic high school this brought
the public secondary schools out on strike. Troops had to be
brought in to keep the students from attacking the Catholic school.

In 1979 there was a special budgetary allocation from the national infrastructure for San Félix, the low-income side of the
city. Unfortunately, this did not work out to redress the balance,
since the CVG then designated all its regular spending program
for the Puerto Ordaz, or high-income, side of town; then the
CVG, lacking ready projects and the staff to produce them, used
the San Félix money for a rather slapdash program of asphalting
streets without proper preparation or drainage systems.[11]

During this period, back in Caracas, a small group of staff—
all women—at the CVG division of Human Development took
it as their mission to work within the agency to try to redress the
balance. They succeeded in getting the CVG to build six new
schools, and they arranged for libraries in the existing schools.
One of these social planners told me in December 1981, with
indignation, how the religious schools built at the CVG's expense
were given air-conditioning and luxurious fittings, while the
blackboards for the public schools were so bad that the man who
was going to install them said he was ashamed; she managed to
divert the elegant blackboards meant for the religious schools.

This image of the planner as guerrilla skirmishing within an
institution dedicated to the interests of the haves in order to cap-
ture some resources for the have-nots will recur a decade later in
the planning office established in the city.

The atmosphere in both the CVG and in its city changed radically when oil prices suddenly rose in 1973. The price change
which created a crisis for U.S. automobile drivers created a different kind of crisis, a crisis of overload, in Venezuela. Venezuela
had for decades been an unusually rich underdeveloped country;
now it was an underdeveloped country with problems of how to
deal with its wealth almost as severe as Saudi Arabia's. Much of
it went into the Guayana. The Venezuelan Investment Fund, cre-

ated in 1974 to invest the surplus oil revenues, put 72 percent of
its total grants and loans into Ciudad Guayana. In the five years
after the oil price rise, more than ten billion dollars worth of the
country's OPEC riches went to Guayana.[12]

The centerpiece of the new Guayana development program
was "SIDOR'S Plan IV"; the plan for expanding the steel mill
fourfold, from 1.2 million to 4.8 million metric tons capacity
from 1974 to 1978. (The new plant was also far more modern
technically than the old; it was built with attention to environmental issues to meet stringent emissions standards and finished
in pastel hues.) In addition, plans were announced to increase the
electrical production capacity of the Guri Dam by raising the
walls 52 meters and adding ten new generators. The state-owned
aluminum company bought out most of Reynolds's share in its
plant and added 70,000 tons of capacity; meanwhile a new aluminum company ordered a plant of 280,000 tons.

The system simply could not cope with it all. There were
hundreds of contracts to manage at any given time. There were
bottlenecks in every direction. Some of these were technical; for
example, the innovative technology for producing reduced iron
ore turned out not to work. There were problems of recruiting
trained personnel and problems of training personnel on site.
Even such elementary things as the production of gravel generated
bottlenecks. Cement delivery was a big problem. The main production sources were on the coast to the north; it was proposed
to truck the cement down until someone calculated the number
of trucks that would be required, and it was clear at once that the
cement would have to be carried round by ship. Cement was
finally imported—from Cuba.[13]

It turned out that the funding available, large as it was, was
inadequate for the projects planned. Siderurgica del Orinoco
(SIDOR), the agency in charge of the steel plant, resorted to
short-term loans at high interest rates from foreign banks. There
was political patronage and mismanagement. In 1982 the steel

mill produced only about 2 million of its 4.8 million tons of capacity, and it was reported that "company officials say the full production figure will probably never be realized. In 1981 the company lost over $500 million. As oil prices dropped, the bottom dropped out of the steel and aluminum markets."[14]

During the oil-boom heyday of "Plan IV" and "Plan V" everything combined to push concern for the city into the background. In the first place was the very magnitude of the industrial projects and the sums of money involved. The hundreds of contracts to be written, tendered, and managed, the sums of money to be disbursed, and the crises and bottlenecks to be solved were simply overwhelming.[15] In the second place, the new head of CVG at this time, replacing General Alfonzo Ravard who had moved up to the nationalized oil company, was an engineer named Gamboa who had previously been in charge of the steel production branch of CVG: his base of experience was, therefore, around the needs of the steel mill which, as we have seen, had all along had a rather uneasy relationship with the city planners. Finally, planning itself was first given a less visible position within CVG and then failed to survive a move to the site. The planning department in Caracas was eliminated. Gamboa announced that he was moving to Ciudad Guayana and expected his staff to do the same. He did appear in Ciudad Guayana, although retaining a suite at the Tamanaco Hotel in Caracas. In the end, none of the planners moved to Ciudad Guayana. "Planning practically ceased to exist."[16]

Meanwhile, the city was overwhelmed by projects and the people who accompanied the projects. There were crash housing programs, but they could not seem to produce housing nearly fast enough. At one time CVG bought an overage passenger cruise vessel which was anchored in the Orinoco and used as dormitories for professional personnel. There were terrible transportation problems, with traffic jams at the Caroní Bridge every day.[17]

In August 1975 the Chamber of Commerce called an important meeting with the director of the state steel mill (SIDOR) to discuss the impact of the new industrial program, Plan IV, on the city's residents. The managers of SIDOR stated that their industrial planning included daily commitments for the next five years. However, from the director's point of view, planning the city's housing, transportation, schools, recreational areas, commercial zones and health care was not the responsibility of the steel mill. According to the legal mandate, urban planning and the allocation of public services were tasks for other divisions of the CVG and separate government ministries.

In 1975 the municipal council declared Ciudad Guayana a crisis area because of the increased demand for public services. Acrimonious remarks about the indifference of the CVG toward the welfare of San Félix frequently made headlines in local newspapers. A Guayana paper *El Luchador* ran this headline August 22, 1975: "Decretan en Estado de Emergencia Ciudad Guayana" (State of Emergency Decreed in Ciudad Guayana). After hearing the new industrial expansion plans of SIDOR the Chamber of Commerce asked that the CVG recognize a state of emergency in the city, not what one might expect to follow an announcement of an economic plan to bring new employment to the city. As a result of persistent conflict with the CVG, the municipal council refused to move from its older building on the plaza in San Félix to Alta Vista, the new site planned to house local government offices.[18]

The unfilled positions in Urban Planning gradually became filled. There was a considerable turnover. Planning per se was in any case rather subordinated to the initiatives held by Programming and Budget, headed by an economist, which set out the housing programs and let the contracts.[19]

The problems of the city were not, strictly speaking, lack of funds. It was the institutional apparatus that was unable to deal with the issues. In 1976, of the sums budgeted for urban development, the CVG succeeded in spending only 27 percent; in 1979, just under 29 percent; in 1980, 14 percent. Only in 1981 did it succeed in spending nearly the whole (92 percent) of its budget.[20]

An administrator in the CVG's Department of Studies and Investigations mused about it all:

> It is becoming the function of planning to create the administrative infrastructure to serve the national planning office. If it hangs together or not no one asks. . . . When we worked on Plan V the industrial programs existed; the others weren't ready. The spigot opened up. When the objectives coincide and resources are ample, the spigot opens. . . . The urban design people were overwhelmed. Everything was contracted out. . . . When you have lots of construction projects going, you don't need planners—and when dividends are down, planning becomes active.[21]

The argument is that urban planning on the grand scale, urban planning as the Joint Center team understood it when they were "planning Ciudad Guayana," is something done when the resources for building are lacking. When the resources pour in, planning goes by the boards.

Today, with oil prices down and Venezuela in a serious recession, the city has run out of steam. Now the rebuilt planning department in the city has found a role reminiscent of that played by the social planners who back in the sixties had induced the CVG to build some schools and had diverted blackboards for them. The city planner who took me around when I visited Ciudad Guayana in 1983 sees himself as an "urbanistic guerrilla." Like a guerrilla, he is short on power and material resources; like a guerrilla his strength lies in conviction and maneuverability. He describes an occasion on which "somehow" he was invited to an

occasion at which all the big wheels of CVG were meeting with
an important corporate executive who had a great deal of capital
to invest and who wanted CVG to let him finance housing and
services for his workers. "I feel like a cockroach at a dance." He
doesn't volunteer; it would evidently not be appropriate for him
to intervene. But then someone says, "Well, here's the planner
here; what do you think?" He makes a modest proposal: Well,
you need a school of course, but the school has two shifts; why
not have your workers' children in the morning and others in the
afternoon? And you want a health center; why not share with
others? thus gradually working the corporation out of a position
around a specialized enclave, and into an incorporation of the
workers and their services into the city. "You need to propose
partial, concrete solutions. Don't fight on general but on specific
issues."[22]

A greater distance from the center of institutional power has,
in some ways, given the reorganized planning department some
new kinds of freedom. Since these planners are not, now, a major
instrument of institution-building and industrial promotion, their
predictions are not so constrained by the needs of institutional
presentation. The head of the CVG's planning office on the site
told me that the 1963 projection of a population of 415,000 by
the year 1975 came about because of overoptimism on every
front:

> They overestimated the capacity to invest; they overestimated
> foreign investment; they overestimated the will of the Vene-
> zuelan government to put the project as a priority; they over-
> estimated the forward-linked complementary industries—many
> of which located nearer to markets; meanwhile, they did not
> understand the relationship between formal and informal parts
> of the economy.

But he says the overestimation was a way of demanding more
budget, and they still use roughly the same methods of projection.

But, he told me also, they now do a set of variations—tendencies, more optimistic and more pessimistic. [23]

One of the problems that was engaging this planner at the time of my visit was the remodeling of an overelaborate subdivision laid out by CVG in its expansive period and now too elaborate and too far from the Center to complete. Another was negotiations with the general purpose of trying to regularize the tenure of at least some of the poor families who had built squatter shacks near the water tank. And it was in the spirit of a guerrilla in the bureaucracy that this planner brought out a report —Ciudad Guayana after 1980—which while starting politely with a recital of "achievements" soon launches into a recital of problems:

- In 1977 investment per capita was thirty-nine times greater in Puerto Ordaz than in San Félix.
- In the past five years, CVG invested in the city only 4 percent of what it invested in industry.
- The concentration on heavy industry does not produce jobs for women.

These general criticisms are followed by an analysis of the shortages of housing and of hospital beds. [24]

Back in the Joint Center days the planners had seen themselves also as representing the interests of the mass of the population within the development corporation. But their work had also been a tool of power. Now that the urban planners are rather decoupled from power, the advocate role comes forward more strongly.

In the meantime, when I visited in 1982 I found a new head of CVG who was personally very close to the new head of the municipal council. Thus, although the council continued to hold out for its old location on the eastern side of the city, it and the CVG had drawn closer together. The municipal headquarters had been repainted and air-conditioned. A secretary for public relations had been brought in. Every Wednesday the CVG planners met with the technical staff of the municipality to share information and coordinate their activities.

The president of the municipal council told me in January 1982 that there were a number of reasons for the improved relations between the CVG and the local government. One, of course, was the personal tie between himself and the new head of CVG. Another, he said, was development itself. Although the CVG still clearly dominates the city, bit by bit the various national agencies were putting their offices in the zone and beginning, not without resistance, to assume responsibility for various urban services. The CVG is not the only power or the only source of funds. This makes it more, rather than less, easy for the municipality to go to the CVG with a proposal for a project and ask the CVG to pay.

He believes, however, that the *mano dura* (strong hand) of the CVG in the beginning was probably necessary to the development of the city. Furthermore, its hand is still strong: it confronts the local municipality as a dominating institution and conduit of resources.

The CVG planners and the municipality are still separate powers. Neighborhood groups may appeal to or negotiate with either and, as in the early period, are likely to turn to the municipality. Direct action by citizens outside the plan has by no means disappeared; indeed there have been a number of invasions not only of vacant land but of publicly built vacant dwellings, including the invasion of a body of housing by a group of doctors.[25] But the city is no longer, in planning's view, "the site" of the future; it was coming to be the social context within which planning had its being.

Notes

1. William L. Porter, "Commerce as an Element of the Urban Form" (CVG, DEPI, file no. E-86, October 1963, Mimeographed), 27.

2. Alex Ganz, interview with author, January 2, 1984.
3. Nathan C. Fitts and Philip E. Beach, "The Economic Situation of the Centro Comercial Alta Vista and Recommendations for CVG Action" (CVG, file no. B-77, December 1964, Mimeographed), 4.
4. María-Pilar García, letter to author, June 11, 1985.
5. William A. Doebele, "Recommended Policies for Land Tenure on the City of Santo Tomé de Guayana" (CVG, file no. A-15, September 1963, Mimeographed); Arthur Fawcett, "Implementation of the Physical Plan" (CVG, DEPI, file no. E-94, November 15, 1964, Mimeographed), 3–5; "Policies Plan for Ciudad Guayana: A Summary of Recommendations by the Joint Center for Urban Studies Guayana Project Staff for Urban Development Policies to Be Adopted by the Corporación Venezolana de Guayana" (CVG, file no. E-93, January 29, 1965, Mimeographed), 15–16.
6. Penfold, "Urban Transportation."
7. Norman Williams, "Notes on the Alonso Report" (CVG, file no. F-15, June 12, 1962, Mimeographed), 2.
8. Anthony Downs, "Creating a Land Development Strategy for Ciudad Guayana," in *Planning for Urban Growth and Regional Development,* by Lloyd Rodwin et al. (Cambridge: MIT Press, 1969), 213–14.
9. CVG, Gerencia de Planificación, "Las inversiones de CVG," 13–14.
10. William Garcia Insusti, "La huelga oxida a Sidor," *Bohemia,* August 23–29, 1971, 6.
11. Interviews with CVG planners in Ciudad Guayana, January 5–6, 1982.
12. Diehl, "Venezuela's Force-Fed Industrial Center."
13. Ganz, interview with author.
14. Diehl, "Venezuela's Force-Fed Industrial Center."
15. Ganz, interview with author.
16. Interview with CVG planners in Ciudad Guayana, January 6, 1982.
17. Ganz, interview with author.
18. David S. Daykin, *The Venezuelan Guayana Corporación and Urban Development in Ciudad Guayana: A Case Study of the Impact of State Enterprises on Urban Housing Policies,* Institute of Latin American Studies Technical Papers Series, no. 27 (Austin: University of Texas, 1980), 4–5.
19. Interview with CVG planners in Ciudad Guayana, January 5, 1982.
20. CVG, Gerencia de Planificación, "Las inversiones de CVG," 16.

21. Johanna Glass de Lopes, interview with author, Caracas, January 7, 1982.
22. Claude Brun M., interview with author, Ciudad Guayana, January 6, 1982.
23. Ibid.
24. Brun M., *Ciudad Guayana más allá de 1980*, 9.
25. Eduardo Castañeda and María Nuria de Cesaris, "Movimientos vecinales y participación de la ciudadania en Ciudad Guayana" (Paper given at the Tenth Annual World Congress of Sociology, Mexico City, August 16–21, 1982), 6.

Chapter 5

The Political Basis of Urban Design:
A Correspondence and a Comment

What follows is an interlude in the argument of the book: a correspondence between myself and my brother on the appropriate basis of urban design. We worry about the degree to which designers have the right to design *for* others. My brother argues that the good city is the outgrowth of a political process in which the community shapes its physical environment. Finally, looking back, I argue that the city can indeed be seen as the physical manifestation of the community, *as politically constituted,* at that time and place.

In early 1963 my brother, James Redfield, came to visit me in Venezuela. James is a classics scholar, then, as now, a member of the faculty of the University of Chicago. The occasion of the visit was personal—my husband's sudden death in a car crash—and most of what we talked about was personal; however, the city and the planning of the city were the context of my life, and we looked together at the city and talked about the planning enterprise.

A few weeks after James returned to Chicago, I got a letter from him, undated, which began by telling me about a seminar paper he had been writing on the *Odyssey*. After using this as the springboard for some comments on varying attitudes toward death, James's letter switches subjects. The next topic is the question "whether policy can have any effect upon the necessities of environment"—the potential of planning.

I have just finished reading Tolstoy's *Resurrection*—we're teaching it this year in the college—Tolstoy of course is totally depressed about the power of men to transform the society which has put them where they are. Tolstoy, I think, would find the Guayana project a sublime example of his theorizing; all this self-important planning which seems to result in exactly what would have occurred without planning or any intervention. For Tolstoy this occurs, as I understand him, because people are incapable of acting for the good of other people when those other people are out there, distant facts or statistics, part of a structure; under these conditions, however, they justify their political organizing and managing. The managers are really only pursuing their own good, status, money, pleasure, the exercise of pride. So it often happens that their activities, so absurd by any standard of the public good, can be immediately understood when we ignore the self-justification of the managers and ask, how does this policy contribute to the comfort or self-importance of the managers?

Tolstoy then goes on to say that people can act for the good of others only when they themselves have a personal stake in the well-being of others, that is through love, and love can occur in very small groups like a family, a school, a revolutionary cell. I think Tolstoy underrates the possibilities of politics, where quite large groups may act toward what they recognize as a common good. Politics is not based on anything as intense as love, but it can, when healthy, have a corporate spirit which has something of the same effect on action. But it does seem to me that he rightly sees the impossibility of working for goods which are not our own.

I wrote back.

San Félix
Estado Bolívar, Venezuela
May 15, 1963

Dear James,

Your letter both interested and moved me. I have been lately reading Hannah Arendt, which for me is very hard work, like reading a foreign language over which you have only mediocre command, but persevering because from time to time I have in that the same experience as with your letter—of suddenly realizing what it is I think.

I hope that Socrates' slave found pleasure in that experience—it was never clear to me that he did. . . .

What impressed me the most was your Tolstoyan analysis of the Guayana project, I suppose partly because to one of my training it is so shocking to make use of the word "Love," and because in thinking about it I felt clear immediately that it was the correct word, whatever the euphemisms that sociologists and anthropologists employ. I had an interesting time trying out your analysis on several people. First, I tried it on the Padre of San Félix—Do you remember him, with the El Greco face? You will not be surprised that he found it correct. For him the only solution to the enterprise is physical confrontation of the Planners and the People—"convivencia." Then I tried it on a couple of the urban designers who happened to turn up here about that time.

This was interesting. Willo (von Moltke) said rather vaguely that it seemed to him correct for "the social part"; another young designer put it more clearly when his comment was, "What does it mean, to 'do things for people'?" and went on to make use of the analogy of the relationship between composer, performer, and audience. So I see that the urban planners, mostly architects in background, conceive of themselves as producing a "work of art," or one of those "cultural objects" which Hannah Arendt describes as "what will last through the centuries." People, they think, will benefit from this work of the mind precisely because it is superordinate to the people who will be using it at any given time.

Putting the matter this way seems to raise a number of interesting problems which I have not yet sorted out in my own mind and can't seem to.

The city which the planners plan will be more of a work of art than the city would be without them—assuming the thing works at all. Will not future generations be grateful for the art in and among which they live? And even if they are not grateful, is not the world somehow better anyhow, just as one might argue that Mozart has a cause for being even if no one ever listened to that music.

When I put it like this, I find it hard to argue with the designer, but still somehow my spirit rebels.

Hannah Arendt, in the essay I read last night, makes use of two categories: (1) the work of art, or "cultural object," and (2) kitsch, stuff made to be consumed. To think about the city as a work of man seems to me to require a third category— those works of man which are neither consumer goods, nor perduring works of the mind like a Mozart symphony, but which are in a more primitive way perhaps expressions of that same impulse to create—of man's immense vitality, and his drive to create a world around him, something not too far off from what the anthropologists mean by culture.

A Mozart concerto is certainly something more than the flute songs of the Fox Indians. Should the Fox Indians then be taught to listen to Mozart instead of tootling their songs? A Rembrandt is better than any child's painting; should art appreciation be substituted for the paintpots and easels of the nursery? To what extent should the people of Guayana be given a city which is a work of art, and to what extent should they be allowed to make their own world?

I suppose I wouldn't have drifted into anthropology if I did not find delightful these naive works of collective creation.

And I suppose I feel it is a bit selfish for the planners to try to monopolize the creative process in growing a city in a place to which they have not even any sense of belonging. Still, I would go along with the designers in agreeing that (assuming they succeed in making their plans operational) the result is likely to come closer to "cultural object."

An ambiguity is introduced by the planners themselves in claiming to be planning *for* people. A Mozart may write *for* a given occasion or audience, but I think the true artist is always pretty clear that that is an extra: that the art is for itself, whether or not it finds an audience.

This same ambiguity, raising many of the same problems in less developed form, is, of course, present in architecture.

A further ambiguity on the other side comes about through the fact that no one lives in the city (read culture in the anthropologist's sense) which he himself helped to create; except to a minimal extent the future generations will have inherited their world from *someone* else. Why not some competent American planners?

Well, I don't know.

This brought from James a longer letter, an essay in the form of a letter.

June 18th, 1963

Dear Lisa,

Your letter raised and reraised all kinds of questions, some of which have been knocking about in my mind for quite a while. I'd like to write you a nice coherent essay on the relation between art and society but I don't have any nice coherent thoughts on the subject. So I'll explore a little. I find it particularly interesting to try to say something to you on the subject, because you are involved with society first and art second, whereas with me the emphasis is the other way.

This year I taught in the College Humanities III . . . the one author all the students wanted to buy without reservation was Croce. Croce defines poetry as a synthesis of image and feeling, so that the image (story, metaphor, character) exactly expresses the artist's sense of it; this Croce calls a lyrical intuition. . . .

Croce calls this "the ordinary concept" of art, and while his language is sometimes puzzling I learned from my students that he is right at least about that. It is a very hard notion to argue with, but, like you "my spirit rebels." There are certain consequences to Croce's position. In the first place, there can be no true critical standard, no gradation between the good and the better. The aim of the artist is to produce art, to produce this characteristic unity of images, this sense of finality. Once he has done this his work is art, and that is all that can be said about it. . . .

In the second place, art *qua* art has no relations to history; both its sources and its results are irrelevant to it. The artist's biography should be irrelevant to our sense of his work, nor are we entitled to consider the effect of the work on its audience. Croce would agree with you that "Mozart has a cause for being even if no one ever listened to that music"; he would go further; he would say that if Mozart had never written his music down his status as a composer would be exactly the same. Once the work is complete in the mind the artistic activity is over; anything else belongs to the history of economics.

Now I take Croce's view as characteristic of modern attitudes toward *fine art*. I think it is a dangerous point of view, and I think we start to see the danger when we talk about arts unlike lyric poetry, arts which are clearly in some practical relation to their environment, arts like architecture and city-planning.

I observe that the great modern architects—Wright, Sulli-
van, Corbusier, von der Rohe, and so on—tend to be terrific
eccentrics intellectually, with a passionate sense of their mission
to remake society, to create a new world order, a new pattern
for human life. This eccentricity—which doesn't seem to do
their architecture any good—is the result, I think, of the strain
imposed upon them by the apparent need of the architect to
maintain his status as artist while still serving the community,
still creating buildings of some practical use. The greatest minds,
I think, respond to this strain by asserting that society should
be subordinate to art, that human life should be rearranged so
that it fits comfortably into their sense of space. A Corbusier
block of flats is (I'm guessing—you'll know more about this)
primarily a plastic creation, an arrangement of concrete and
glass whose initial justification is aesthetic. A theory of society
is then invented to justify the plastic creation; people ought to
live in a way suited to the building and if they don't, if they
ignore the nurseries and the internal shops fail for lack of custom, if the people who live there continue to commute into
Marseilles, it is the people who are at fault.

Lewis Mumford has written a lot about this in the *New
Yorker,* but in those articles—I haven't read his books—I have
not seen a discussion of the underlying aesthetic which produces both buildings and theories. The problem is a modern
one—that is, since 1600—and has, I suspect, its roots, like so
many other things, in the rise of middle-class and eventually
industrial society. The demands of such a society on its members tend to be anti-artistic; a large-scale money economy and
atomised division of labor tend to value the useful at the expense of the expressive. So the artist feels that organized society
is his enemy; he goes off to the Lake District or Tahiti, he
becomes a Bohemian who never pays his rent or a dependent
who seduces the wives of his aristocratic patrons or locks himself in a cork-lined room. Much more important, he develops

an aesthetic which asserts that art, *fine art,* has no obligations
to society; he creates for the artist a separate society in which
art speaks only to artist. So in our time art for art's sake has
become the slogan, explicit or implicit, of all the artists who
are doing any decent work; those artists who have attempted
to relate their work to society, lacking a secure intellectual
foundation, have usually produced one of two kinds of non-
sense: either a messianic art—futurism, Yeat's notion of the
theater—which asserts that it is the duty of the artist to remake
the world in the image of his special and superior revelation,
to bring about "a new rebirth of wonder" in Ferlinghetti's
phrase, or party-line art—social realism, didactic novels—which
assumes that art should be the tool of some worthwhile social
purpose. And I could add a third fallacy, the notion that since
the world is a certain way, it is the duty of the artist to reflect
it, whether we judge the world chaotic, as in America, or
progressive, as in Russia. None of these schools seem to have
considered the possibility that the world of art and the world
of society are not separate, that there is only one world in
which we all live and in which all our activities take place. I
suggest that our sense of any single activity can only be made
rational by our sense of the whole.

I would start with Aristotle, usually a convenient starting
point for anything, but particularly useful here because in Aristotle's philosophy there is no notion of *fine art.* He is groping
toward it in the *Poetics* but the idea is so alien to him that he
never quite makes it. In the *Ethics,* for example, Aristotle describes three kinds of activity: theoretical, science, in which the
aim is the contemplation of truth; technical, art, in which the
aim is some product or situation, pots for the potmaker, health
for the doctor; or practical, prudence, in which the aim is living
well, so that the activity is itself the end. The relative status of
theory and practice is a sticky question which doesn't really
come up here; I would start from the relation between pru-

dence, that is: politics and ethics, and art or technique. For Aristotle there is no problem; technique is clearly subordinate. The proof of this is that we hire other people to handle our technical problems but not our prudential problems; we are happy to have other people cut our hair or repair our plumbing but we want to make our own moral decisions; we would feel that turning them over to someone else was an abdication of our essential humanity. As Plato says the ship-captain can get you to Egypt but he doesn't know whether or not it is a good thing for you to go there, and the second kind of knowledge is clearly the most important one.

The problem arises when we start to consider those works of art which are clearly not "useful" in the limited sense suggested above; for Aristotle it starts with Greek tragedy. A tragedy has no purpose other than its own existence; as you I think rightly say: "the true artist is always pretty clear that (the audience) is an extra." Sophocles did not set out to produce a catharsis in a lot of people; his aim was to compose the *Philoctetes*. Yet these works are not moral either; we do not judge the play by whether the motivation of the artist in composing them was good; furthermore, while we look upon morality as open to anyone of decent upbringing we think that the arts require special talents. The easy answer to this problem is Croce's, but I think there are others.

Santayana, in *Reason in Art,* suggests another answer. He starts by pointing out that any "useful" activity may, by being treated as an end in itself, become what he calls "ideal." This term means something like my term above: "expressive." At a certain moment the passion for the object in itself takes over from the use for which the object is intended; at this moment the activity of the artist is not one of service to the environment but of free exploration of the possibilities of the medium. Even objects designed to be of use in fundamentally corrupt activi-

ties can take on ideal values; consider, for example, late Me-
diaeval armour.

What, then, is the relation between "useful" and "ideal"
products? Santayana says that the aim of all art is to "humanize
the environment," to make it responsive to our needs and
wishes. To give an example which is mine not his:

Suppose you are moving into a large bare room with a
window. Your first aim would be to make the room livable
in an animal sense; you might put in plumbing, build furniture,
and so on. In doing these things you are shaping the room so
that it is responsive to you, so that it is an easy, comfortable
place to live. But ease and comfort are not the only human
needs. The blankness of the walls may offend you; you might
run a Greek design around the top of the walls, thus making
the roof seem farther away. This activity is not useful but ideal;
nevertheless you are still humanizing the environment. You
might want to hang a picture—perhaps a picture of the garden
outside the window. The aim of the picture is not to produce
a substitute for nature, but to add to it; picture and garden
taken together from a satisfactory unit. Furthermore, you are
going to have to think about how the whole thing goes together; the picture would have to go with the Greek key design, and the Greek key design with the plumbing. From this
point of view there is no clear distinction between useful and
ideal; the man who sits on the chair and the man who admires
the picture are the same man; he must ration his resources and
energies according to his sense of the relative place of chairs
and pictures in his life as a whole.

Now for Santayana the world we live in is like that blank
room; we begin from nothing and gradually make it livable
through our creations, art, law, custom, religion, all those
things which taken together constitute our culture. There is
this additional point to make; a great work of art, just because
it lasts forever, permanently remakes the environment. Once

the *Iliad* has been written and widely read the world will never again look the same to its inhabitants. The *Iliad* has, in that sense created a new environment for them. So it is not analogous to a product, like a pot, but to an invention, like the potter's wheel. Like an invention it offers not necessity but possibility; we do not have to see the world as Homer saw it any more than we have to make pots; his vision is one of the visions open to us. As civilization grows, as its tradition becomes larger, the possibilities become more various. If, and only if, we continue to dominate those possibilities, to choose between them on the basis of a rational standard of life toward which we are always working, our lives will become not only more complex but happier; otherwise our art, like our inventions, may swamp us.

I like this way of going at it because it demands that we ask what I think of as serious questions. We stop concentrating on formal perfection for example, and start to ask questions like: is Wagner's music consistent with parliamentary democracy? (By the way, I think the answer is yes.) We demand of the art we take seriously that it be consistent with our whole sense of what the world ought to be like.

Santayana's aesthetic seems particularly attractive to me, I suppose, because it works well with the classical art of Greece. There the split between artist and society hardly existed, so also the division between useful and ideal, and between high art and kitch was hardly made. The Greek plays were occasional pieces, written for one performance; sculpture was one of two things: architectural decoration or monuments commemorating victories and deaths; even much lyric poetry was written on commission. Santayana, I think, looks back to this world when he says:

What we call museums—mausoleums, rather, in which dead art heaps up its remains—are those the places where the muses

are intended to dwell? . . . A living art does not produce cu-
riosities to be collected but spiritual necessities to be diffused.
. . . There is genuine pleasure in planning a work, in modelling
and painting it; there is pleasure in showing it to some sym-
pathetic friend, who associates himself in this way with the
artist's technical experiment and with his interpretation of some
human episode; and there might be satisfaction in seeing the
work set up in some appropriate space for which it was designed, where its decorative quality might enrich the scene,
and the curious passerby might stop to decipher it. . . . A
community where art was native and flourishing would have
an uninterrupted supply of such ornaments, furnished by its
citizens in the same modest and cheerful spirit in which they
furnish other commodities. [*The Life of Reason or the Phases of
Human Progress: Reason in Art* (New York: Charles Scribner,
1926), 209-10]

So after all this rather long-winded prologue I come to city-
planning as an art.

People who write about architecture usually observe that a
building is both useful and ornamental; they often seem to
assume that there is a permanent tension between these two
things, that the necessity of being habitable gets in the architect's way as an artist. It is this distinction I am trying to break
down. Take the case of an architect who designs a house for
himself. He will certainly attempt to make that house fit his
wishes, make it, in Santayana's phrase, a humane environment
for himself. He may not worry about heating the ground floor
properly in his delight with the high ceilings and wide stair
wells. But, if we assume that he knows what he is doing, this
means that high ceilings are for him more important than
warm floors. The house is what he wants it to be, and there
is no reason to distinguish between his wish for ornament and
his wish for comfort; he balances the two as seems to him

best. The split arises, I suspect, because architects tend to feel that in arranging comfort (and modest expense) they are indulging the patron, and the problem of the social status of art arises in an acute form with architects and city planners not so much because their work must be lived in, but because their work is nearly all done for a patron and not for themselves. A man who buys a picture buys it because he wants to bring something of the artist into his house (this is also true of Mozart's symphonies); a man who commissions a house, or a people who ask for a city want something in quite a different sense their own.

Suppose that our architect is building not only for himself but for his wife as well; they may have quite different ideas about the desirable qualities of a house. The wife may have relatively little sense of the spatial qualities of a building, she worries, perhaps, about whether the building will be easy to clean. If we assume a happy marriage the final house will be a product of the sort of discussion, compromise, and agreement which governs other important decisions: where to send the kids to school, whether to spend the housekeeping money on steak or beer. And if the marriage is really working the final house will not be an uneasy compromise between them but a product of their joint wishes; the architect will value it all the more because it expresses something larger than himself: his marriage. This is the way I think of successful city planning. A city is the environment and the property of a community; it should express that community's sense of the commodious and the beautiful. Since the basis of community life is not love but justice, or rather justice made vital by occasional love, so the final product will not be reached by pure agreement, but by the rough-and-ready consensus of politics.

There are plenty of arguments against politics as the basis of community action, but they are all wrong. Since Plato at least people have been telling us that we would be better off if we got some expert to run our affairs, a philosopher king, perhaps, if we could hire one, or failing that a city manager with a Ph.D. in Administration. But I think, just as I want to make my own moral decisions, so I want my community to make its own decisions; to give this up is to lose some essential humanity. Politics is living well for a whole community, just as morality is living well for an individual; it is not a means to something else; rather a healthy political life is itself the end at which all acts of public policy aim. This does not mean that the public arts must fall into the hands of the Philistines, any more than democracy means lynch law. Any healthy community must give much liberty to the creative people whom it trusts; sometimes a committee should say, not "this or that sort of building" but "build us a masterpiece; we approve it in advance." But the liberty of the public artist is in the gift of the public, and it is the right and the duty of the public (of which the artist also is a member) to determine how that liberty shall be used.

For this reason I would not make von Moltke's distinction between the "social part" and city planning proper. To inflict on others a city is just as much an impropriety as to inflict on them a constitution or a president. I have an unhappy feeling that this sense, common to experts, that their place in the world is to solve other people's problems for them and then leave the people to adjust to the solution, is the curse of technical assistance projects. To me a technical assistance project should be more like a marriage counsellor, whose function, as I understand it, is to learn from the parties and teach them of themselves, to help them to understand what they themselves really want with the most enlightened part of themselves, and then show them the way to achieve it.

What would this mean in practice? Maybe the place to start is not with roads and bridges or even schools but with local government. Maybe the CVG should be developing as many groups on all levels as it could, encouraging the unions, the party organizations, the church groups, the local councils. Before there can be a community decision there has to be a community. And a focus for community life; some of the money, at least, might go to these groups to spend as they decide. The project can only do its job by being an outsider, a neutral, but it is really doing this job if it is self-liquidating, not in the material sense but in the social sense. Having more people on the site would help, but not if those people simply became the local ruling class. Assistance means service, but a servant can also be a leader; a teacher is the servant of his pupils. Of course the people who live in the city are not the people who are there now, but a community can only grow if it has once been born, and it can only grow healthily if it grows from the inside, not into an artistic pattern created beforehand by members of some other community.

With this burst of metaphor I'll quit. I had something to say and I've said it. Perhaps you have no desire to get such a sprawling piece of work; if so ignore it. Sometime I'll write more about what I am doing here, but it's not nearly as important or as interesting as what you're doing there. I hope you don't get washed away in the floods.

Lots of love,
James

This odd correspondence represents one angle of vision, a single commentary, on the Ciudad Guayana story—not a summation of it. There is much that is left out. The idea of urban design is greatly oversimplified. We see that Croce's "ordinary concept" of art was only one of the ideas which the design team brought to their task. The designers did, indeed, at some level, wish to produce a "cultural object," a "beautiful city." But they also saw their ideas of the city beautiful as being modified by the require-

ments of efficiency in function. How they seized on the predictions of the economists and the transportation planners!
Furthermore, they were anxious to take into account the preferences of ordinary city residents; it was, after all, in 1962 very
advanced practice to hire an anthropologist and to ask her to
provide information on the customs and values of the people.

But looking back at my brother's last long letter I see how
nicely it captures a sense of the city that was entirely foreign to
the Guayana designers: the idea of the city as the outcome of
people struggling to shape their environment to satisfy both their
tastes and their interests: the outcome of the "rough-and-ready
consensus of politics." That was part of the Aristotelian city in
which I lived, the city of community organizations and municipal politicians and the chamber of commerce.

But if we look at matters in another way, we may see the
planning as set in a political context and as constituting a part of
the political institutions. Planning in this view is part of politics,
a special way of doing politics.

"I want my community to make its own decisions," says James.
"Politics is living well for a whole community, just as morality
is living well for an individual." Splendid words.

But "community" is either an abstraction or a social vision or,
more realistically, some combination of the two; in practice, it is
found in both these modes within a particular set of institutions.

What was "the community" in Guayana? What politics could
have been called up to create the good city? Guayana was a place
of hustlers and boosters, of corporate privilege and of struggle
for survival, bound together by competitive collaboration in the
economic process and by a shared vision of progress.

In Ciudad Guayana, in the early sixties, the local institutions
were weakly developed; the national institutions were rich and
powerful. In some ways, the condition of Ciudad Guayana in this
respect was typical of Venezuela in general. Political and economic
decision making tended to be highly centralized. The national

government was collecting about 85 percent of all tax revenues. National ministries performed many major urban functions: a national agency did water and sewers; another national agency distributed electricity; health services were provided by the Ministry of Health or the national Social Security system; roads were built by the Ministry of Public Works. State governments had far fewer resources: the municipalities fewer still.

As national planning came to Guayana, the municipal government consisted of a council with no technical staff, housed in a rather dirty building in some need of repairs on the plaza of San Félix. There were funds to repair an occasional pothole, but not to build streets. Small allocations of pipe and gravel could be made to community self-help groups. There were four or five municipal policemen; they had a jeep, but in the absence of a telephone system, they could not easily respond to crisis. The limited resources available were issued in a notably personalistic way.

The municipal councilors were accessible to the citizenry, in general, willing to be helpful via the modest means at their command, and not incompetent at managing the kind of local politics they were used to managing. However, they had neither the resources nor the experience to deal with a large budget, long-term planning, or issues on a national scale.

In Ciudad Guayana, the situation was atypical in the presence of the national development agency, the CVG, with its control over land and its substantial financial resources from the national government. The hierarchy of power and resources was clearly visible, for example, in the schools. The Ministry of Education ran the largest and best-financed public schools, the state of Bolívar some rather inferior ones, and the municipality a number of rudimentary one-room schools. Meanwhile, the CVG built a number of exceedingly luxurious private schools staffed by Catholic priests and nuns. These certainly aroused envy among those who did not have access to them; they were not rejected as models.

With its institutional resources and its mandate to plan, the CVG had at the outset a substantial capacity to set the program and define its purposes. The investment budget of the CVG was the instrument of shaping the city physically: of creating the physical framework of community. The creation of plans, and their embodiment in brochures and reports was the instrument for defining the meaning of the city: of projecting community interest as a social vision.

While the CVG's vision of community was not entirely shared by those in the existing city, they were not able to contest it. They were unable to do so both for practical and for ideological reasons. The local leadership lacked a resource base in any way competitive with CVG. Furthermore, as shown in an earlier chapter, they lacked an alternative vision. There was general allegiance of persons in all parts of the social structure and of all political groups from Left to Right to the idea of Progress. The idea of community—as in "the nation," "the city"—was joined with the idea of progress and harnessed to a project of development planning of which the city, as it came to be, is the embodiment.

The city that emerged from the design and planning process with its wastefulness, its glaring social inequalities, its pretensions, and its shantytowns was indeed the physical representation of the "community" and its politics.

Chapter 6

Representation

Planners and designers are people, and collectively they constitute social groups. As such, they have social relationships with the world around them. As professional practitioners, however, they deal mainly with various representations of reality: maps, site plans, statistical tables, and the like, each of which is an abstraction of the reality out there. The planners' and designers' social relations no doubt interact with their professional practice to shape both the choice of representations and their interpretation. Nevertheless, it is possible to look at the vocabulary of representation which professional practice makes available at a given place and time as the instruments with which a given group of individual professionals has to work. In trying to understand the Guayana Project it seems particularly appropriate to look at the forms of representation, since the planners and designers were so socially isolated from the world of the site. Representations were not simply the way the planners presented a world, intimately known, in order to achieve some particular effect on an audience; the planners to a substantial degree experienced the city through their own representations of it.

In ordering the vocabulary of representation present in the Guayana Project we follow the dictionary in bringing together concepts that are ordinarily thought of as sharply different—indeed, as relating to quite different realms. "An image, likeness or reproduction in some manner of a thing" or "a material image or figure: a reproduction in some material or tangible form: in latter use *esp* a drawing or painting of a person or thing" seems

111

to locate us in representation as the artist or architect knows it. "A formal and serious statement of facts, reasons or arguments made with a view to effecting some change, preventing some action, etc.; hence, remonstrance, protest, expostulation," puts us in law or politics. "The fact of representing or being represented in a legislative or deliberative assembly, *spec* in Parliament; the position, principle, or system implied by this" and "the aggregate of those who thus represent the elective body" identify a set of political institutions and the social theory which legitimizes them. Yet all these lie, in the *Oxford English Dictionary,* in a continuum of meanings.[1] All are important meanings for planners and designers. All forms of representation are abstractions from reality which bring some aspects forward to the attention and leave some in the background or eliminate them completely. At one end of the continuum the descriptive meaning of the term *representation* is emphasized; at the other, the political meaning. But because it selects and emphasizes, because it makes a statement about the world, a description has political effects to the degree that people attend to it and are influenced by it. And at the other end of the continuum, the institutions that we call "representative" stand as, and are intended to be, in various ways and according to various not wholly compatible theories,[2] descriptions of the society they represent.

In looking at the various forms of representation available in the Guayana Project, the subject is the vocabularies of description, not what is specifically being said. I want to look at the drawings made by urban designers as representing a kind of vision of the urban environment, not with respect to the artistic quality of the drawings or the merit of the designs they show. I want to look at statistical projections as a way of thinking about society and its transformation, not with respect to the accuracy of the statistics themselves or the particular things they tell us about the universe from which they are drawn. Nevertheless, form and content are intertwined. What can be said depends on the language for saying it. That is the interest in looking at representations in planning. The focus here is on the underlying messages carried by the forms of representing.

In figure 1, a sketch done at the beginning of the project, Wilhelm von Moltke, the chief designer of the Joint Center team, represents "the site" of the city. The drawing is done with pencil on tracing paper, cheap material intended for transitory use. The representation is not only schematic but sketchy. This is a working document, a memo to the designer himself to clarify his understanding and an illustration for working discussion with colleagues. Nevertheless, it has great clarity and sense of command, and von Moltke kept it in his files for twenty years.

The sketch represents the site as a whole, from a considerable distance, so that it lies before a viewing intelligence located somewhere in space but in no particular spot. Land forms are represented with that visual sensuousness with which an artist converts a woman's body to the few lines of a curving spine and jutting hip. The works of man are prominently featured and labeled but enter the sketch as visual features. The representation describes the city as a single thing, linear in form, with a series of lumpy shapes both natural and man-made strung out along its flowing axis.

If one were physically present viewing the city in this way, what else would there have been? One was a landscape of sky: an almost overwhelming bowl of unobstructed light beating down without a cloud during much of the year, with dramatically shifting clouds during the rainy season. (The Philadelphia planner Edward Bacon, with whom von Moltke was connected personally and professionally and who came to Guayana in the early period as a consultant on the form of the city, found that he had completely misunderstood Brasília when he learned about it through representations that omitted the sky.)[3] In addition, all sense modalities other than sight are eliminated: the heat, the smell of the baking vegetation, are not represented.

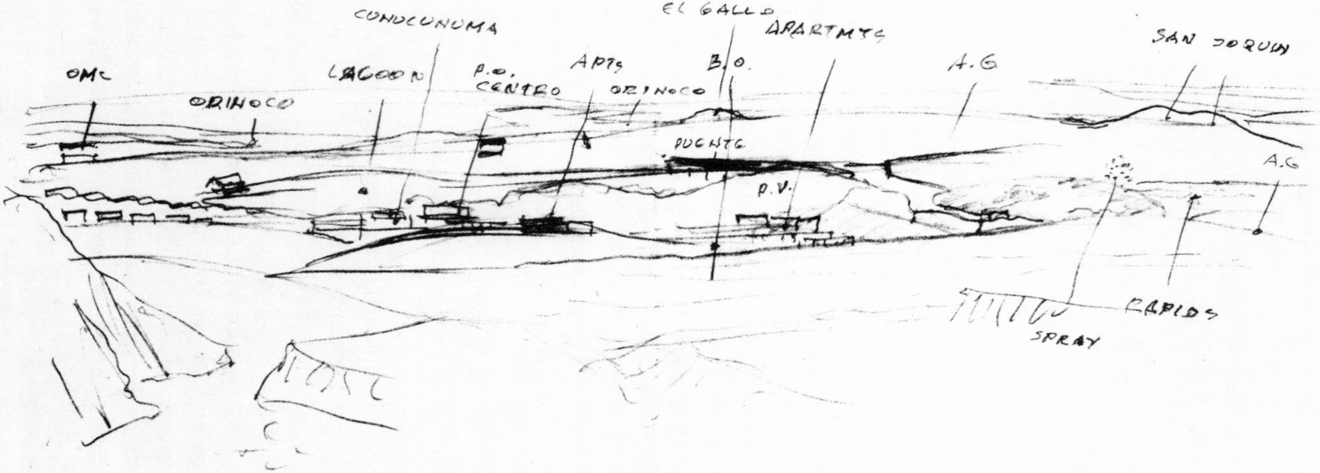

Figure 1

But most strikingly, human purpose and human meaning is taken out of the landscape. The Orinoco Mining Company and Puerto Ordaz Center become forms, along with river and hill.

The urban designer Donald Appleyard came to Ciudad Guayana during the planning period and made a survey of the residents' perceptions of the city. When he published this material later, he commented on the striking differences between the elements important to the urban designers and those important to the residents.

The designers focused on the natural setting.

The urban designers began their work with systematic surveys of the natural terrain around the city to assess its development potential. By trudging and jeeping along the tracks of the Savannah, by boating up and down the rivers, and by viewing the site from helicopters and small planes, they were able, with the help of excellent maps and aerial photographs, to gain a thorough knowledge of the landscape. Every turn in the riverbanks was learned; geological and geographical features were surveyed and labeled from aerial photographs; the alignments of roads, railroads, and shipping channels were noted; vegetation, soils, and special views were recorded. The designers became practiced at drawing accurate sketch maps of the area, sketches on which the rivers stood out above all other features as a framework for locating roads, settlements, and bridges.[4]

The designers put rather less effort on getting a picture of the man-made environment.

The emphasis on the future city and the pressure to make plans for it led to some neglect of the existing city. A land-use survey made at the very beginning of the project was never used and subsequently lost. In consequence, all available maps were either of the existing landscape or of the future city, and it was difficult to tell from them exactly how much of the city had been constructed at any one time. The planners' knowledge, though extensive, placed more emphasis on the landscape than on the existing settlements.[5]

In this focus of attention, the planners were taking a view exactly the reverse of that of the residents of the site.

The inhabitants' maps confined their attention in the main to the urbanized areas. In a city whose pattern of development was fundamentally influenced by two great rivers, both vital to its economy as transportation routes and sources of power, these rivers were virtually ignored.

The surrounding landscape . . . seemed to have little meaning to the inhabitants of Ciudad Guayana. They appeared to see the city as an outpost in an unknown territory, rather than as one embedded in its surroundings. . . . Only when the natural form was useful as part of an urban activity, as a source of economic riches, as a name for a barrio, or as a recreational setting did it appear to enter their environmental schema. . . .

. . . while the inhabitants' interest in the surrounding landscape was low, their knowledge of the urban area turned out to be reasonably extensive. . . . The inhabitants' knowledge of the city was therefore the very converse of the planners' knowledge. In perceptual terms, the inhabitants saw the "figure," and the planners saw the "ground."[6]

More basically, one sees that the sketch has no way of representing human purpose. The elements of the existing landscape, the human as much as the natural, are simply given: they do not represent centers of power, outcomes of struggle and investment, the bases for proposals for change. The sketch converts a city of hustlers, politicians, entrepreneurs, families, and reformers into a pattern of masses and forms and their spatial configurations.

Also during the early design period the staff members of the team made a number of sketch plans for the "form of the city." In these sketch plans, the two rivers, their intersection, and the waterfalls of the Caroní dominate as setting the context for human activity in the planned city. Within this frame, the elements are various activities (residence, industry, commerce) located in space and the transportation links (roads) connecting them. Again, power, purpose, and even the nature of the functional activities and their social and economic interconnections are suppressed from the representation. (Indeed the conventions of such plans with their single-use areas would in themselves render it impossible to adequately represent any real place in which various activities were carried on in a single area.) What emerges is a conceptualization of the city as a whole rendered two-dimensionally as if viewed from a great distance overhead.

Working in Caracas, the planners of course had available to them largely information coming in the same form: maps and aerial photographs of the site. But oddly enough, when they made their trips to the site they very often tried to reproduce the mapping experience for themselves. After taking an excursion around the area by car, perhaps stopping to stand in the plaza or to try out the straw hats in the market, they would often laboriously climb the hill at the eastern edge of San Félix and gaze out over the city, tracing paper in hand.

A version of this kind of simplified "city plan" intended for public consumption is shown in figure 2. Here the various "land uses" are schematically represented in bright colors, the function of which any planner will at once recognize as promotional. (One of today's CVG planners refers to such brightly colored representations derisively as "kites." However, he points out that he could only get agreement on a project to renovate the plaza in San Félix when "the architect came in with the 'kite' with the promenade and the plaza shown in a way which could be anywhere; it sold them completely.")

Even more lively visually is figure 3, taken from the same

CVG publication as the foregoing. Here is proof that it is possible (although perhaps not easy) to represent human purposes in two dimensions. The graphic representation of the Guayana region seems to convey the idea of furious activity focused on Ciudad Guayana. The regional economic resources are identified and roughly located, and the city is conceptualized as a center of economic exchanges. But in this representation, again, the residents of the city have no place; the city is a target—indeed, physically symbolized as such—of the purposes of outsiders.

The representations we have seen all have as their most general purpose that of establishing the whole city as the object of planning. The real place is shown as physical forms and in miniature; the designer might think of manipulating it as a child would his block city.

The next three illustrations (figs. 4–6), in contrast, are representations of the designers' approach to the neighborhood scale of development. These drawings are only three of many plans and renderings produced in connection with a project for a middle-income urbanization on the west side of the river. They are intended, among other things, to display the feasibility and desirability of an urbanization which differed sharply from prevailing practice—in the use of row housing, in the unconventional organization of plots, in the creation of tree-shaded semipublic spaces, in the importance given to pedestrian pathways. It was hoped that this neighborhood, designed early in the planning period, would serve as a model for subsequent urbanization.

Figure 4 shows a view from straight down, but here the purpose appears to be less that of rendering a place into a map, than of showing how a particular plot layout can work. In figures 5 and 6, we are among the (still imaginary) buildings and trees. The neighborhood is very clean and orderly. Few people are to be seen. Furthermore, part of the feeling of airiness is, on examination, due to the fact that the viewer is somewhere in the air,

Elementos dominantes de la ciudad Ciudad
Guayana tendría cuatro focos principales: el centro
de la industria pesada en Matanzas; el centro
de la ciudad en Alta Vista; el centro recreacional en
Punta Vista y el viejo casco de San Félix. Estos
focos estarán unidos entre sí por la principal
arteria de la ciudad la Avenida Guayana.

	Matanzas: área de servicios para la industria
	Alta Vista: centro de la ciudad
	Punta Vista Parque Caroní
	San Félix, centro comunal
	Comunidades residenciales
	Metales y maquinaria pesada
	Servicios portuarios y áreas industriales
	Puertos

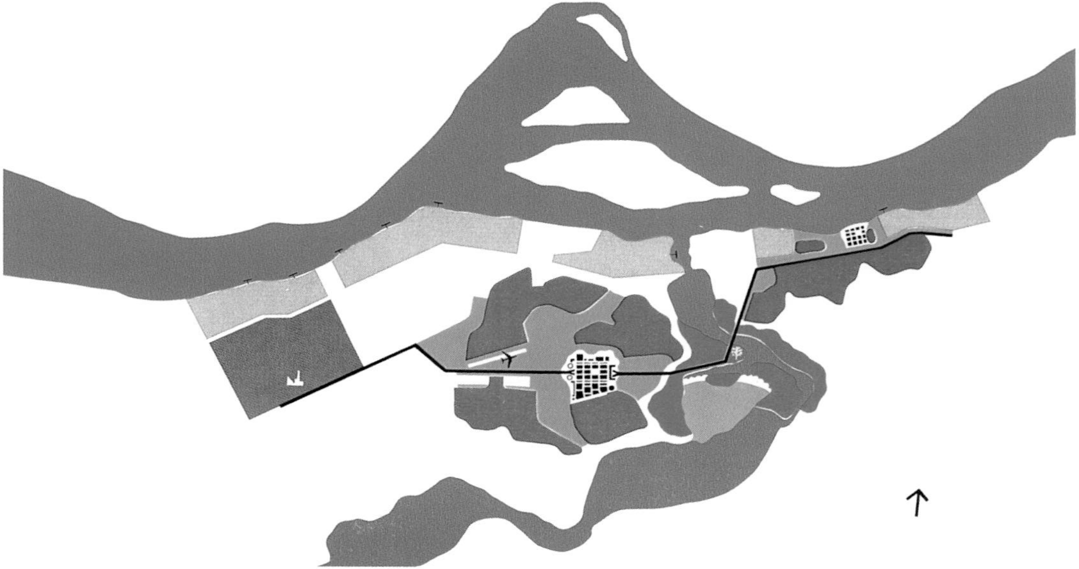

Figure 2

La región de desarrollo de Guayana dentro de un radio de 100 Km a partir de Ciudad Guayana y de su industria pesada se encuentran yacimientos de mineral de hierro, petróleo y gas; bosques; zonas agrícolas fértiles; y un gran potencial hidroeléctrico.

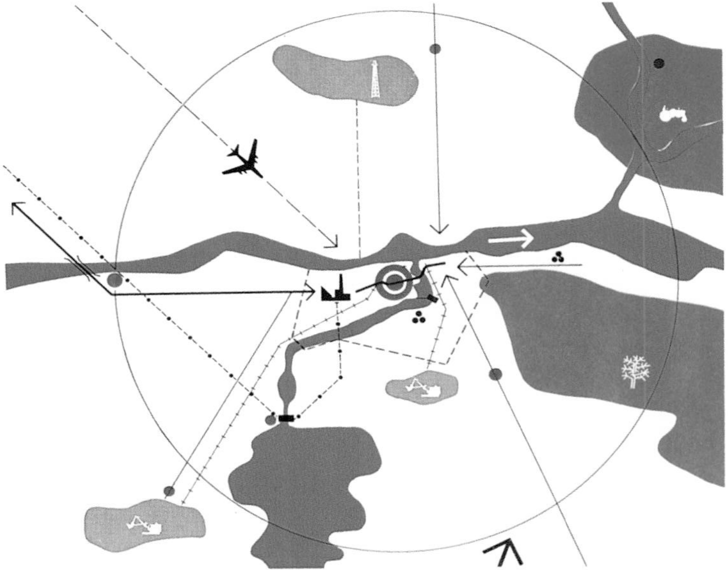

Figure 3

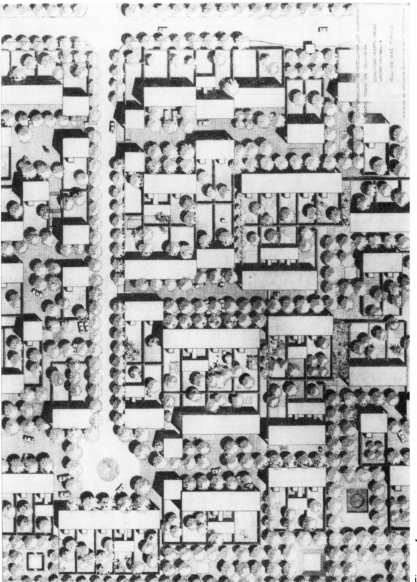

Figure 4

A COLECTOR

B CALLE

C PATIO COMUNAL
GRUPO RESIDENCIAL—VIVIENDAS CONTINUAS

D BARRILA VERDE CONTINUA

Figure 5

Figure 6

Figure 7

not in the sky looking down, as in the early city plan views, but not standing on the pavement either: perhaps floating a little bit.

Finally, in a rendering of the proposed new market for San Félix (fig. 7), we are, at last, practically on the ground among the people of the city. But we are in a market that is almost as airy and unpeopled as the urbanization preceding; a market so uncrowded would surely be on the way to financial ruin. Stall keepers appear to be calmly arranging their vegetables while, presumably, enjoying the cool of the high shading roof. Competitive struggle, the passions of entrepreneurial creativity, have no place in this rendering. The market has become, like the model urbanization, a place to enjoy the shade.

These representations, in contrast to those of the city as a whole, show people; indeed, they are in a sense human centered. The esthetic qualities of the masses and spaces are less the subject than is the cool comfort they create as a setting for human use. But the role that persons play in these renderings is that of users: they are using and, one is to understand, enjoying the use. It may be helpful to recall that in discussions of urban design the topic of people in relationship to the built form usually appears under the heading of "user needs." The point to be made about all this is that the concept of user needs and its representation in the sort of renderings we have here is a selection from a much wider range of possible human relationships to the built environment. We should notice not only what the representations show, but what they don't show. We see people using; we do not see them making, controlling, profiting from. We can extrapolate from these representations to issues of taste; we do not easily derive from them issues of interest. These renderings of places introduce people, residents of the city, quietly enjoying the designers' work, not contending with each other within it or contesting the planners' right to arrange things.

Drawings and plans were the representations of a design perspective on the city. More characteristic of planning is the use of statistics, and in the Guayana Project these were the preferred representational tool both of the economists and of the "social planners." The use of statistics is compelling, practically and persuasive. "Numbers" appear clear and unequivocal. It is possible to match categories via numbers: the number of households is set against the number of housing units; the number of classrooms is related to the number of children. There is a factual look to numbers; things have been counted.

But behind this facade of factuality there are problems. We all understand counting: "One potato, two potato, three potato, four . . .". But there is a difficulty in establishing the categories of counting. When is it appropriate to say, "You cannot lump together apples and oranges?" and when is it appropriate to count "fruit"? Statistical modes of presentation organized around the evaluation of future outcomes tend to approach the issue of value by way of monetary transactions, either past or potential, sincewe do not have an alternative generally agreed upon system of measurement. Thus the statistical mode of presentation is particularly appropriate to projects which are set in a framework of financial profitability and tends to introduce financial criteria into the analysis of projects to which it is applied.

Table 1 represents the Guayana Project industrial development program as drawn up by the Joint Center economists in March 1962. Without dealing with the specifics of the program's plausibility, let us look at this table as a form of representation: as a way of describing reality. What are the characteristics of this particular mode of representation?

It is a form of representation that looks very precise; there are numbers, which suggests that things have been counted. But it is at the same time extremely abstract. The entities totaled are not things at all but high-order abstractions of events—making, selling, paying, etc. Even in the left-hand column what we find is not factories which might appear on the landscape as discrete buildings with people inside making things, but "industry groups"—a categorization of economic activities. "Investment" and "value of output" are even more highly abstracted representations of monetary flows which are themselves, given the nature of money in modern society, highly abstract. "Labor force" is an abstraction that generalizes a large number of different sorts of persons involved in different ways in complex social arrangements and drawing from these activities different kinds of remuneration. "Value added" is a concept that involves differentiating two categories of inputs into the productive process: already-manufactured intermediate goods (like sheets of steel in a refrigerator factory) or services (e.g., insurance) from those factors of production—land, labor, and capital—which enter directly into the manufacturing process. The latter, valued at their rate of reimbursement, constitute "value added." There is no doubt that this concept has its uses in helping us to think about the difference between a Mexican-border assembly plant and the steel mill of Guayana, but what a lot of abstracting goes into the figures in the "value added" column! Isn't labor also an "intermediate input," produced into semifinished form by a variety of agencies from mothers to technical schools? Doesn't it make a difference which inputs are being used, at both sides of the conceptual divide, and who produces them? What is the implication of lumping together the returns to land, labor, and capital (surely in our day, as in that of Adam Smith, evidently disparate and even competing persons) as a single category of "valued added"—to particular individuals? to society? and in what sense? Surely the meaning of such a category is to set up a (highly abstracted) society-as-a-whole as referent, passing over the deep divisions and conflicts of interest that characterize real societies.

Behind this table lies concealed a bog-land of epistemological issues and their ideological implications, perilously spanned by an elaborate set of intellectual constructions operationalized into conventionalized conversions. But the form of representation, the numbers in neat tables, associates it all with the objectivity of

TABLE 1. Guayana Project Industrial Development Program, March 23, 1962

Industry Groups	Value of Output (in million dollars)			Value Added (in million dollars)
	Total	Domestic	Export	
Metals				
Furnace and rolling metal products	1,200	800	400	600
Ore reduction	525	—	525	262
Aluminum	250	125	125	115
Magnesium	12	6	6	5
Manganese	48	24	24	19
Subtotal	2,035	955	1,080	1,001
Machinery				
Construction machinery	80	80	—	38
Hoists, cranes, etc.	40	40	—	19
Oil field machinery	120	120	—	62
Machine tools	70	70	—	45
Mining industry machinery	80	80	—	43
Other machinery and equipment	200	50	150	108
Fabricated metal products	150	100	50	76
Subtotal	740	540	200	391
Chemicals				
Calcium carbide	10	10	—	5
Elementary phosphorous	35	—	35	19
Ammonia	32	—	32	17
Chlorine	3	3	—	2
Caustic soda	3	3	—	—
Subtotal	83	16	67	43
Construction Materials				
Refractories	5	5	—	3
Cement plant	6	6	—	4
Brick and tile	2	2	—	1
Concrete pipe	10	10	—	6
Concrete blocks	4	4	—	2
Concrete slabs	8	8	—	5
Asbestos cement siding	10	10	—	5
Subtotal	45	45	—	26
Forest Products				
Pulp and paper	44	44	—	18
Rayon	15	15	—	9
Saw and planing mill products	30	30	—	13
Plywood	1	1	—	1
Subtotal	90	90	—	41
Grand Total	2,993	1,646	1,347	1,502

Investment (in million dollars)	Labor Force (number)	Power Requirements (in M. W.)	Freight Generated (in thousand tons)	Space Needed (in acres)
1,100	15,400	1,500	6,000	1,200
300	6,250	1	15,000	250
250	3,500	880	500	1,750 (?)
20	200	36	20	100
24	510	80	80	20
1,694	25,860	2,497	21,600	3,320
n.d.	3,100	n.d.	n.d.	15
n.d.	1,600	n.d.	n.d.	11
n.d.	6,000	n.d.	n.d.	24
n.d.	2,300	n.d.	n.d.	14
n.d.	4,000	n.d.	n.d.	20
n.d.	8,000	n.d.	n.d.	26
n.d.	5,000	n.d.	n.d.	25
300 (est.)	30,000	8 (est.)	100 (est.)	135
17	200	57	100	20
20	585	50	100	20
30	450	5	400	15
{15	{110	{19	45 / 50	{4
82	1,345	131	695	59
6	400	n.d.	160	70
45	175	n.d.	300	90
2	195	n.d.	50	39
5	700	n.d.	20	70
1	220	n.d.	20	44
2	530	n.d.	200	130
2	556	n.d.	10	110
63	2,776	2 (est.)	760	553
70	2,000	9	200	100
5 (est.)	650	10	10	33
2	1,500	{1	n.d.	187
1	104		n.d.	10
78	4,254	20	210	330
2,217	64,235	2,658	23,365	4,397

counting and to the representational practices of "practical" business.

In table 2 we see the industrial program used as the basis for projecting the total population of the city at successive time periods in the future. The method employed is clearly explained in an accompanying note.

> The point of departure, . . . was the estimation of the economically active persons required by the heavy industry and mining industries which form the basis of Santo Tomé's economic structure. These requirements were based on production targets for iron and steel, reduced iron ore, other metals, heavy machinery and equipment, electrochemicals, construction materials, pulp and paper and forest products, established in line with an analysis of world and Venezuelan demand, Guayana Region resources, and a preliminary evaluation of feasibility, taking into account scale, linkages, transportation, location and other factors. . . .
>
> The estimates of the economically active persons engaged in the other industries and services required to support the population deriving its livelihood from heavy industry and mining were developed in the first instance using industrial distributions of the economically active population of various Venezuelan cities. From the total of the economically active population obtained by this method, preliminary estimates of the total population of Santo Tomé were computed. In addition, a refinement of the estimates of the economically active population engaged in the "other manufactures" sector was obtained by estimating the number of persons required to produce that part of manufactured consumer goods which it was estimated would be produced locally. . . .
>
> The estimates of the economically active persons for each-industry group in the "other manufactures" sector were then derived by dividing the gross product by the gross product

TABLE 2. Projection of the Active Population, Ciudad Guayana

	1966*	1970	1975*	1980
Total Population	115,000	248,669	415,000	656,606
Total Active Population	36,184	82,931	146,000	221,379
Total Heavy Manufacturing Industries	7,855	22,668	43,794	64,235
Basic metals	5,041	13,050	18,660	25,860
Machinery and equipment	2,033	8,100	19,100	30,000
Chemicals	—	303	764	1,345
Construction materials	781	1,215	2,516	2,776
Forest products	—	—	2,754	4,254
Mining	1,100	1,500	2,000	2,500
Subtotal: Heavy manufacturing and mining	8,955	24,168	45,794	66,735
Agriculture	1,720	2,487	2,502	2,516
Other Manufacturing Total	4,206	10,474	19,553	28,629
Industrial sector	1,660	4,607	9,775	14,942
Foods and beverages	454	1,143	2,993	4,842
Footwear and clothing	758	2,213	3,434	4,655
Textiles	6	19	76	132
Furniture	61	176	1,164	2,151
Graphic arts	74	215	526	836
Petroleum by-products	5	15	34	54
Others	302	826	1,548	2,272
Artisan sector	2,546	5,867	9,778	13,687
Foods and beverages	1,036	2,465	4,354	6,244
Footwear and clothing	1,443	3,225	4,876	6,525
Furniture	67	177	548	918
Construction	8,066	13,861	22,372	33,233
Electric energy, water, sanitation services	302	770	1,577	2,492
Trade	4,234	9,240	16,640	29,079
Transport	1,815	3,850	8,603	14,539
Services	6,886	18,081	28,959	44,156
Subtotal: Agriculture, services, and other manufacturing	27,229	58,763	100,206	154,644

*Interpolated
Date: December 19, 1962
Author: A. Ganz and J. Phillips
Prepared by: C. Fuentes
Approved by: A. Ganz

per worker. The latter figures were obtained by increasing the 1959 national average for the respective industries at a rate of 3.5 percent per year in the industrial sector and 1.0 percent per year in the artisan sector. The revised estimates for the "other manufactures" industries were then incorporated in the estimates of the economically active population, and new totals were computed. From these new estimates of the total population of Ciudad Guayana were made for the years indicated.

There has already been occasion (chaps. 3 and 4) to comment on certain aspects of this methodology. The need for promotional optimism directed those who made the table to list among industries to be located in the Guayana every kind of desired industry which seemed at all possible. It thus becomes unclear whether these population figures are a prediction—basis for programming the city—or a set of targets; the very promotional requirements that led to the ambiguity made it difficult to discuss the issue forthrightly, even though it was apparent enough to lead to subsequent modifications of the figures.

But at this point, we are looking at the table as a form of representation, as a mode of describing reality. The fact that this way of arranging the statistical story is quite conventional should not lead us to assume that there is nothing to be said about it: rather the reverse. Intellectual categories arise out of social arrangements and in turn help to make the arrangements seem the only possible ones, and thus to maintain them. What are the characteristics of the particular mode of representation and its categories before us here?

The center of the stage is held by "heavy manufacturing" and "mining"—in real life rather than as statistical categories, large corporate entities with their centers of management and their stockholders elsewhere. A secondary role is played by "other [local] manufacturing." The people of the city are represented as the direct expansion of the scheduled industries. The industries, expanded to labor requirements, expanded to total population—this describes the city. People are represented via their prescribed economic role; if they do not have such a role (as by being unemployed and resorting to selling snacks in the street) there is no place for them in the picture. The conceptual categories that power establishes by treating some activities as desired and belonging as of right and others as out of place is expressed in the statement "No matter how well they plan the city, people keep coming in and messing it up"; these categories are represented even at the level of statistical description.

As time went on in the Guayana Project, there was a great deal of "data-gathering": activities which at least strongly resemble the counting of things. There were surveys of income and employment and of household expenditures; there were surveys of the numbers and characteristics of dwelling units; there were surveys of residents' migration histories and of their opinions on various matters.[7] In 1980 the CVG issued a rather thick volume of the statistics it had amassed on the Guayana region.[8]

As a way of thinking about the use of statistics at this level of description, let us take two examples (tables 3 and 4) from a study by John MacDonald[9] which used the analysis of social surveys in the city in 1965 and 1975 to evaluate the planning and implementation of the Ciudad Guayana Project.

The data are presented in terms of a sample stratified by the kind of residential area where the persons responding to the survey were living: an officially sponsored urbanization (urbs.) versus an irregular settlement (barrio), the latter, in turn, substratified into "houses" and "shanties."

One set of statistics is an attempt to say something about levels of welfare; the other is an attempt to say something about the social processes involved in migration. Both sets of statistics are interesting ones. But we must simply notice how much abstraction goes on even at this level of detail. A "household" (as I have reason to know from trying to design a survey in such an area)

TABLE 3. Monthly Household Income, 1965 and 1975 (in percentage of households)

Bolivars	Urbs.		Barrios				City Total	
			Houses		Shanties		1965	1975
	1965	1975	1965	1975	1965	1975	(N = 496)	(N = 899)
0–999	15	32	56	54	75	78	57	53
1000–1999	42	39	37	35	22	20	31	33
2000–2999	23	20	5	8	2	1	7	10
3000–3999	12	6	1	2	1	—	3	3
4000 and over	8	3	1	1	—	—	2	1
Total	100	100	100	100	100	100	100	100

Note: Reprinted, by permission, from John Stuart MacDonald, "Planning Implementation and Social Policy: An Evaluation of Ciudad Guayana 1965 and 1975," in *Progress in Planning*, ed. D. R. Diamond and J. B. McLoughlin (Elmsford, N.Y.: Pergamon Press, 1979) 11:84.

TABLE 4. Critical Assistance between Relatives or Friends (in vertical cumulative percentage point scores)

	Post-1964 Arrivals					
	Active Kinship Links			Active Friendship Links		
		Barrios			Barrios	
	Urbs.	Houses	Shanties	Urbs.	Houses	Shanties
On the way	184	214	221	48	63	44
On arrival	106	131	177	67	77	61
Subtotal	290	395	398	115	140	105
Later crises	47	35	58	16	17	16
Total	337	430	456	131	157	121
Total minus housing help	334	404	424	131	157	121
Total minus followers	290	355	387	131	157	121

Note: Reprinted, by permission, from MacDonald, "Planning Implementation," 11:64.

is an extremely fluid and not sharply bounded affair; people join and leave and while around contribute varying proportions of their earnings to any common pool. "Income" is equally or more problematic in an economy where many people are not on any regular payroll, and where there are earnings in kind from petty agriculture. It is easy to imagine the variety of stories which have been generalized and coded to produce tables 3 and 4.

In contrast to the drawings, the statistical representation is discontinuous. It does not represent the connections. It is like one of those connect-the-dots pictures with which we all played as children. But, like the connect-the-dots picture, the connections are implied: in this case, not simply by the way the various numbers are arrayed with respect to each other but perhaps even more importantly by the way in which they were generated in the first place, by way of the categories of counting.

Those in charge of the Guayana Project of course understood the limitations of maps, drawings, and statistics in representing the social or human aspects of the city. Thus, it was from the beginning part of the project planning to include a sociologist (or anthropologist) as part of the planning team. I was that anthropologist, and it is now my task to explain why, during over two and a half years on "the site," living in the evolving city and reporting on it to the planners, I emerged with such a strong sense of having been able to introduce very little into the planning process.

When I arrived in Caracas I found that the planners who had been working there for some months had developed a set of categories within which they hoped I might work. The first-order categories here were items on the planning agenda—e.g., design of open spaces, planning for commercial facilities—and from these were derived agendas for the "sociologist"—"Analysis of social problems existing or likely to develop in areas devoted to open-spaces; social function of open spaces in an urban living pattern; family structure and activities, modes of using leisure time . . ."

or "Analysis of social problems existing or likely to occur in connection to the development of commercial areas; analysis of changing shopping habits; analysis of time-distance factor, distance to market, number of trips to market . . .". I rejected these categories with a sense of indignation, indeed of defense against a kind of violation, which I can still distinctly recall. They were planner categories, and not only were they nonanthropological, but they were unlikely to feed into the sorts of holistic descriptions and analyses anthropologists are trained to value and to make. Furthermore, anthropologists are trained to work with categories which in some sense arise out of and express the categories of experience of the people being studied; these categories were not of that character. So I insisted that I must go down to "the site," find a place to live, begin working as a participant observer, and develop categories in the process. I hoped in this way still to be useful to the planners, and I believed in the long run only in this way could I be useful to them.

Never, in the more than two and a half years I was there, did I arrive at a set of categories and problems mutually satisfactory to the planners and myself, or even satisfactory to either one. Instead, I seemed to move between two conceptual worlds, two sets of problem definitions, unable to find a set of categories and concepts that would join them. In 1963, after a year and nine months, I wrote a satirical account of life as an intermediary between two reference groups, groups not only different from each other but in direct conflict at many points. I wrote:

> The anthropologist is brought into the technical assistance scene as a solution to a general set of difficulties; those arising out of a gap created by cultural difference, social barriers, and general lack of channels of communication between the outsider technical experts or planners and the "natives." But the anthropologist—now brought in—does not do away with the gap. Rather he now presents himself within it as an individual

who wanders across a sort of social no-man's land trading with the combatants on both sides and collecting and disseminating information like those double espionage agents who flourish on the boundaries of international relations. His position is ambiguous and problematical.[10]

What was it that I had to trade on either side of that gap between planners and citizenry? For the people in the growing city, I could provide little bits of information, sometimes specific—Could you find out what happened to my petition to build a filling station on the corner?—and sometimes more general, as in informing the parish priest or some of the municipal councilors as to the planning going on in Caracas. Once I had the pleasure of teaching my neighbors to make and circulate written minutes of the commitments made in a meeting with representatives of the CVG.[11] With respect to those who were paying my salary, the Joint Center Guayana Project, the issue of what was my product seemed more serious.

The variety of materials with which I had to work may be suggested by scanning a journal entry for one day, April 1, 1963. The original notes are very rough and in a mixture of Spanish and English. I have added and edited only enough to make the words, if not the sense, understandable.

A.M. Trip to see Carlos re finishing house of Señora Vegas.

Visit to supposed "kindergarten" back of the medical center which turns out to be a dispensary.

Trip to Campo Caroní (housing near the dam for the CVG employees) to make an appointment with Señora Freddy Hernandez.

Sticking my head into the newly painted "Junta Consultiva para el desarrollo integral de la Zona de Hierro" (Consulting Committee for the comprehensive development of the Zone of Iron), find the Secretary, Señor Hurtado, in. Whistling through his teeth in his excitement, he shows me a list of groups meeting there: something every night this week—public employees, Lebanese, Press Club, Hunting and Fishing, etc., etc. Asks me if I am a "doctor" and excitedly types out an invitation to the opening meeting of a Promotion Committee for the Caroní Cultural Center (Athanaeum).

P.M. Another trip to Carlos re Señora Vegas.

Interview with Mrs. Freddy re her kindergarten which went broke because people didn't pay and there were enough poor families sending so she didn't like to charge them ($30 a month, plus a half bolívar each way transport). Not a graduate, but full of zeal; she showed me a hand-copied curriculum guide for kindergarten, also kindergarten rating sheets put out by the Ministry of Education. Knows of no present kindergarten besides that run by the nuns.

P.M. Discussion with Trina about baptism of Henry: card in file. "Modern people" have quantities of godfathers and godmothers. Hers is a typical social-mobility mix: doctors from the Social Security Hospital, chauffeurs from Social Security, teachers from El Roble [adjacent neighborhood], main godmother a beauty parlor operator; her assistants also down.

Enthusiasm among Anna and her friends for new classes in La Laja [my neighborhood and Anna's]. Ministry of Agriculture Home Demonstrators two nights a week for women, two for girls. Seems to have been put into operation by Peraza, according to Trina.

Italian grocery enlarging greatly.

Hortensia's house being plastered.

Señora Morillo getting zinc roof and cleanup of wall.

On arriving at CVG Urban Development office find Carlos coloring the river blue on a map. He looks up ruefully and says he has been captured by the mentality of Caracas and feels that colors on a map are the real thing.

Who are all these people? What is the relevance of all this to planning a city?

As to the first: Carlos is a naturalized Venezuelan architect on the staff of the development agency, working on the site. Señora Vegas is a Caracas social worker, well placed in the dominant political party, who during this period was considering taking charge of social programs on the site; thus Carlos and I, the two Joint Center staff on the site, were involved in getting the house across from mine remodeled for her use. (In the end, she did not take the job and thus did not come.) Señor Hurtado is a local political figure with obvious cultural-promotion interests. Mrs. Freddy Hernandez is the wife of a CVG engineer who at one time ran a nursery school. Trina is a paraprofessional nurse, wife of a storekeeper, and my neighbor; Anna is another neighbor, a teen-ager; the buildings mentioned are in my barrio.

Each of these people is in my mind an actor in a drama of longer duration which is playing itself out before me. Señora Vegas's house is part of the story of how much energy on the part of the development agency goes into organizing the city for their own comfort. Señor Hurtado's Centro Cultural Caroní is part of the story about how the traditional regional elite become incorporated into a city with a political and economic base largely outside their control. The investigation of the kindergarten is part of an attempt to inventory social programs on the site. Trina's is a story of social mobility; as I lived there, I watched her "out-grow" her illiterate storekeeper husband and leave the neighbor-hood. The classes in my neighborhood sponsored by one of the town councilors is part of a story on the workings of the political system at the local level. The physical improvements in three buildings are part of a story about incremental building without official sponsorship or financing. Carlos's comment about the map becomes part of a story, later put into an article[12] about how the critical gap came to be not between planners and people but between those on the site and those in Caracas.

My world was full of continuing stories of people's lives which interlinked with each other to make larger stories: about social mobility and the transformation of traditional social groupings into a new class structure, about the development of the political system, about the social functions of planning.

Out of these stories I made written contributions to the work of the planning team back in Caracas.

On the one hand, I reported on activities in the developing city: the verbal equivalent of the planners' sketch maps. An example: a listing, with brief descriptions, of existing and incipient social programs on the site.[13] This listing was itself a modest attempt to alter the planning process. "Social planning" back at headquarters seemed to consist of proposing a set of social programs on the basis of criteria arrived at among the planners themselves, without reference to existing activities in the city. I wanted a more consultative and adaptive process, and thought my list would help. I also responded to particular issues of physical planning by generalizing as to the relevant patterns of belief and action of people at the site. An example of this is a memorandum reacting to a set of questions about the design of residential areas in which, among other points, I try to explain the working-class pattern of combining wage labor and urban life with keeping chickens and growing plants as "a desire for continuity as well as . . . a real functional adjustment to a situation in which wage labor is transient and undependable."[14] I drew up (on request) plans for more complex programs of social investigation than I could myself execute alone.[15] I gave detailed accounts of how certain programs were actually working (or not working) down on the site: a review of the steps that had to be gone through to get permission to build a community center was presented as a model of the bureaucratic barriers to development; a look at the complexities of loan processes in the sites-and-services project showed why people were not building under the program. And I commented, often critically, on the planning process.

Social planning should not be thought of as separate from, as added to, the rest of the CVG program. The entire CVG program is one of effecting gigantic social changes. . . . If social planning is to make any sense in this situation, it must mean that the CVG must subject its whole program to scrutiny from the point of view of what will be involved from people and towards people in carrying it out.[16]

In all of these communications or written representations there seems to have been a single underlying theme: This is not "the site" of planning, but a city in embryo; the inhabitants are not dependent on outside intervention to enter a process of development but are themselves making history via individual and collective struggle.

Far from waiting apathetically for the government to "do something for them" the people we have met seem to be only waiting for the government to fire the starting gun and cut the tape. They act with great energy when they are permitted to.[17]

Let the CVG planning division try, as much as possible, to stay out of the business of "telling people how to run their lives." Let the social planners not begin by drawing up a blueprint of some ideal state of social organization, according to our present viewpoint. Let us rather work as learners, mediators and clarifiers.[18]

We cannot conceive the situation . . . in which "modernizing" inputs are being fed in, more or less exclusively from the outside, especially e.g. by the CVG. The society on the site is as much self-transforming as being transformed. The CVG is only one competing source of "intellectual leadership."[19]

Even the more utilitarian memoranda previously cited have this as an underlying theme. One shows that chickens and fruit trees are a reasonable way of coping with economic uncertainty, not cultural backwardness; another shows that there are lots of social programs in the city already, even without the CVG.

But in looking back at this period, I see that I very much lacked a suitable form for representing my view of reality. The words I put together lacked, on the one hand, the "factuality" of what could be counted: they were in this respect less powerful than the tables of the economists. On the other hand, they lacked the compelling immediacy of graphic art; they had less power than the representations of the designers. If I told my stories with the vivid concreteness of the specific they appeared as particulars, not as showing general issues about which policy should be made. If I generalized them into categorical form I was supporting the very position which, at bottom, I wanted to call into question: the right of the planners to define the issues. In the end, as a member of the project team, it was the generalizing mode I more frequently adopted.

In 1964 when I prepared to take my family back to the States the Joint Center proposed to support me for a year to write a book about the project. I took this as an opportunity to find the form to represent my reality. It would be a brief, a statement on behalf of the people to whom I had become committed, seen both as underdogs and as the agents of historic transformation. It would define the problem in my terms, rather than in those of the planners. And it would make my world on the site vivid, present, real to the planners, the outsiders. It tried to do this by presenting—I hoped with something of the raw primary impact they had had on me—some of the experiences of that world. I cited Pablo Neruda's sarcastic lines for the book's epigraph:

> Everyone has been contented
> with the sinister presentations
> of shrewd capitalists
> and systematic women.
> I want to speak with many things . . .[20]

I tried for a representation of an alternative view in a book I called *The View from the Barrio*,[21] which described "the site" as a society in transformation, without a planner in sight.

Could I have found better forms of representation while I was still involved in the project? Moving into the generalizing form of the planning memorandum made my ideas relevant—but it converted an alternative view to another opinion on the issue. Looking back at them, I like the vividness and three-dimensionality of my accounts of bureaucratic process at the site—but I notice that none of these made their way into the permanent files of the project, and this may indicate that the specificity which I see as their strength rendered them ineligible as authoritative evidence for policy.

In retrospect, I believe that I could have made more than I did of the vignettes of personal history and collective struggle which were my "stories" from the site. I would have had to develop these into generalized accounts of social process and trace the implications of process in the present for the character of the city in the future. I would have had to be more daring and more explicit in developing a picture of the city as evolving rather than as planned from above.

Perhaps also I could have used my position as a resident of the site and participant in the world there to arrange meetings and interviews for the planners with some of the more active persons in the evolving city. I did a little of this informally, but I could have tried to do it more systematically. Had I done so, of course, I would have moved more closely toward the political meaning of representation.

Politics, too, can be thought of as a way of representing—in a descriptive sense—the character, interests, and desires of a group of people. In her interesting essay on the diversity of ways in which the concept of representation has been used in political theory, Hanna Fenichel Pitkin points out that in some of these usages the descriptive element is very strong. Representation may be the mystic embodiment of the will of the people, representation may be seen as authority to act on behalf of, but representation may also be thought of in terms of resemblence; the composition of an elected body should, in this view, be like that of the electorate. Or the representative may be seen as required to be an adequate representative by accurately depicting the wishes of his constituents. She suggests that there is, in these discussions, an underlying polarization on the representative role which she calls the "mandate-independence" continuum. "Should (must) a representative do what his constituents want, or what he thinks best?"[22] The position a particular theorist adopts on this range depends, she tells us, on his "metapolitics." The issue is this:

> The more a theorist sees representatives as superior in wisdom and expertise to their constituents, the more he will stress the need for independent judgment. The more he conceives of political issues as having correct, objectively determinable solutions accessible to rational inquiry, the more he will incline to independence. . . . The more a theorist stresses the national interest, the welfare of the nation as a whole, the more he will object to binding the representative closely to his constituents' demands.
>
> The more, on the other hand, a theorist sees a relative equality of capacity and wisdom between representatives and constituents, the more it will strike him as arbitrary and unjustifiable for representatives to ignore the wishes and opinions of the people. The more political issues strike him as involving irrational commitment or personal preference, choice rather than deliberation, the more necessary it will seem that the representative consult the people's preferences and pursue their choice. The more a theorist thinks of personal or local interests as needing defense against a threatening central power, the more he thinks of the representative's function as critical of government action rather than as initiating it, the more likely he is to favor a mandate position.[23]

With these comments in mind, what could we say about the role of politics as a form of representation in the Guayana Project?

We would have to say, first, that at the local level there was a reasonable element of representativeness in the political institutions. The membership of the municipal council was certainly not drawn equally from all sections of the community; they tended very much to represent the local business elite, both in social composition and in the positions they put forward. The one more working-class member of the council at the time I was there spoke to me frankly about his self-consciousness on this score. Thus we would have to say, at the outset, that if the local municipal council had had more power in the planning process this would have tended to benefit especially the local commercial elite and rather less the ordinary working-class citizen. But the social gap between the local councilors and the general electorate was not great and the council was quite accessible to contact with and influence from the mass of citizenry. Indeed, this accessibility was dramatized for me one day when on coming to the municipal offices I finally located the council chairman hiding behind a post to avoid the myriad of importuning mothers who had heard that one of their number had been given an allowance to buy school books for her children; now they all wanted the same.

In addition, there were a number of local neighborhood groups which in various ways represented the wants and needs of the citizenry. In 1977 national legislation mandated the creation of neighborhood associations, and by 1982 eighty-one such associations were legally registered in the city, sixty-two of them in San Félix and nineteen in Puerto Ordaz. Representatives from these bodies sat on a commission on zoning. There was also a conservation board created by legislation on the environment and educational committees mandated by national legislation on education.[24] These formal institutions for bringing the citizenry into government were still in the future during the early planning period. "Representation" only reached to the level of municipal government. But even then (in 1963) there was a great deal of activity at the local neighborhood level involving self-help public works like the installation of water lines, school rooms, and sports fields, in the process linking local interests with the resources (gravel, pipe, school teachers' salaries) available at the municipal level. These neighborhood organizations were grouped together in an advisory board sponsored by the council chairman and meeting at the municipal council building. In present neighborhood associations it is the more socially established who get involved in such issues as zoning and development location; in the case of lower-income residents the supply of basic services is of higher salience. In my time in the city, living in a neighborhood with a great deal of community organization going on, it was clear that even at the most local level representation was not complete; a large part of the neighborhood never participated in the community organization, and the more active participants were likely to be the better-established economically.[25] Nevertheless, we may generalize that both now and during the early planning phase there are and were a number of institutions at the local level that we may describe as being, in several ways, representative of the local population, even if not always in contact with national power centers.

On the other hand, the agency planning the city at the national level, the CVG, was in a very different relationship to the people living in the city. The agency was composed of people very different from the local citizens in social class and in professional formation. It was physically distant and intentionally inaccessible; General Ravard believed that giving out information on the plans would only lead to problems. The agency was not required to respond to wishes of the local citizens. Nor did the planners think of their plans as embodying the needs of the local citizens of the present, for it was the future city which was the focus of planning and the present political structure at the national level which represented the context of the project.

Thus the social differences between the development agency professionals and the people of the city were linked with the ideology of planning itself to place the planners clearly at one end of the continuum of meanings of "representative" that Pitkin outlines. The planners were certainly very unlike the people of the city, so they could hardly constitute good representatives in the sense of likeness. And on the other hand, the idea of expertise rationalized a sense of representing higher and more general interests than those of the current population.

Those at the top of the CVG saw their distance from and lack of responsiveness to the people of the city as entirely appropriate. They were not planning the city for *those* people. They saw themselves as planning the city in the interest of the nation as a whole and the future residents of the city. Their optimistic, progress-focused view of the future made it possible to think of the future population of the city not only as very much more numerous than the present, but as different people altogether. To respond to the wishes and needs of the present residents was thus to respond to particularistic interests distracting from the goal of building the city of the future for the people of that future and meeting *national* goals.

In addition, the position of the planners was obviously such as to maximize their adherence to the beliefs which, Pitkin tells us, lead to the "mandate" position. They saw themselves as superior in expertise to the ordinary citizens. They saw issues as having "correct, objectively determinable solutions accessible to rational inquiry." The project was set up to stress the national interest, the "welfare of the nation as a whole."[26]

Pitkin tells us that there are two underlying rationales for governmental leadership in society. One is seeing that people's affairs are well looked after. The other is "providing for all . . . an enduring common enterprise which perpetuates their achievements and enlarges their vision and their sense of themselves."[27] The Guayana Project promised both: a national project enlarging the vision of the participants, executed in the framework of rational problem solving.

Thus the way the politics of the Guayana Project represented reality made for a very deep separation between the people and interests of the city at the present on the one hand and the people and interests of the future city on the other. In the present were the municipal council and the local neighborhood organizations and direct action by individuals and groups. The issues were concrete and immediate: water lines, access to land. Thinking about the future was governed by the ideology of progress and of economic development. The issues were general and national: growth, modernity, progress. The representation of the city in politics thus inevitably subordinated issues of daily life and individual realization to those of the project as defined by CVG in Caracas.

When we look at the modes of representation employed in the Guayana Project, we see a great deal of congruence. The modes of representation are diverse, but just as a melody transposed into different keys and variously orchestrated is still the same melody, the designers' graphic representations, the economists' statistical projections, and the political institutions all emphasized the abstracted city of the future as a perfected implementation of the general welfare and downplayed the existing city of the present as a set of particular problems and interests. All privileged the planners and the corporate institutions—public and private—which they represented as the source of initiative and transformation. My vision, because of my professional background and because of my working situation, was divergent, seeing the city of the future as evolving from the present one and the interests of local institutions as needing affirmation and expression; however, I was not able to represent that vision in a way which made it really usable in the planning framework.

One way of explaining the congruence between the planners' modes of representation and the political institutions is to say that politics drove planning. The political mode of representation was not on the same level as the others; it constituted a system of power, capable of driving other institutions and their images into conformity with the interests which dominated it. But this would be, I think, an oversimplification. The planners believed in what they were doing; they saw their professional practice as state-of-the-art. Planner representations and political institutions supported each other and shared in a set of common ideas about development. To the degree that politics drove planning and shaped the ways in which planning represented the situation, this congruence had been achieved through processes well antedating the Guayana Project; a kind of professional culture had evolved in the context where planners worked for governments and with a commitment to vested economic interests. The forms of representation in the Guayana Project were state-of-the-art professionally.

In subordinating the present to the future and the local to the national, the structure of the political and planning institutions ensured that certain interests would dominate in the long run. Choices as to the form of the evolving society were being made. It would be a society dominated by large, corporately organized, high-technology institutions of production. It was the central mission of the CVG to attract and privilege these corporate investors. The city was principally their city. Indeed, in the years following the early planning period the close interrelationship between national government and corporate industry was to become a single interest in the form of the nationalized oil, iron, and aluminum corporations. "Big business" was then not simply the major concern of government; it was the business of government. But in the planning for and the imagery of the future it was already clear that large corporate business would dominate and small business would have a distinctly subordinate role. The path was being cleared for a technocratic elite and below them a sharp differentiation between those workers with places in the big companies and their fringe benefit systems and the large underclass outside the corporate system and marginalized by its privileged institutions.

Thus what was at stake in the representation of the city was not simply the interests of the people in the present versus the interests of the future residents. The struggle between local and national, present and future, also constituted a present version of a potentially far-reaching struggle between big business and small and between the state and the corporations on the one hand and the rest of civil society on the other.

In this potential conflict of interests, the political institutions of the time and place were bound to privilege government and the large corporations. The national government, with its ties to the large corporations, was strong; the local government, with its base in the local business and professional community and, to some extent, the rest of the voters, was weak. But the planners also contributed to the outcome. There were, first, the forms of representation their practice involved. Urban design focused on the pieces of built environment which the government would sponsor other than the component of the city—actually much larger—that was being created by a myriad of private firms and persons. Design focused on the visual appearance of things, not on their cost, ownership, or profit-yielding consequence, and it thus yielded a view of the city in which interest and competition of interest was invisible. Economics saw the large corporate investors as the economic base, other firms and individuals and their activities as derived from and dependent on the heavy industries. Here, too, institutions and the struggle between them was subsumed into statistical aggregates of output. Planning in general treated the inhabitants of the city in the present as representing particular interests that should yield to the creation of a richer, nobler, more "modern" future; in any case, the forty-five thousand persons on the site at the moment would appear a tiny-handful against the numbers to come. It might have been my role to have reinterpreted the present as a small model of processes and issues to be addressed into the future, but I did not succeed in finding the language of representation to make that happen. Finally, planning as a process was one which managed information selectively to the disadvantage of the small and the local.

Prediction and sharing of information as to intent took place at the top. The planning system was even more opaque to the locals than the rest of government, as shown by the fact that when the local businessmen wanted to deal with the planning of a major road, they had to take it to their political contacts rather than to the design team. Planning aided, glamorized, and rationalized the reorganization of the environment around large corporate investors.

Notes

1. *Oxford English Dictionary,* s.v. "representation."
2. Hanna Fenichel Pitkin, "The Concept of Representation," in *Representation,* ed. Hanna Pitkin (New York: Atherton Press, 1969), 1–23.
3. Edmund Bacon, *Design of Cities* (New York: Viking Press, 1974), 235.
4. Appleyard, *Planning a Pluralist City,* 18–19.
5. Ibid., 21.
6. Ibid., 22–23.
7. In addition to the various publications of the CVG, see Appleyard, *Planning a Pluralist City;* David Samuel Daykin, "Urban Planning and the Quality of Life in Ciudad Guayana, Venezuela" (Ph.D. diss., Vanderbilt University, 1978); María-Pilar García, *Planificación urbana y realidad social: Distribución espacial, sistemas de actividades urbanas y vivienda de la población de escasos recursos de Ciudad Guayana,* 2 vols. (Caracas: CVG, 1976); idem., "La Guayana Venezolana: Otro caso aleccionador," in *Las Truchas: Inversión para la desigualdad?* ed. Ivan Restrepo (Mexico City: Centro de Ecodesarrollo yEditorial Oceano, 1984); María-Pilar García and Rase Lesser Blumberg, "The Unplanned Ecology of a Planned Industrial City: The Case of Ciudad Guayana, Venezuela," in *Urbanization in the Americas, from the Beginnings to the Present,* vol. 3, ed. Richard F. Schaedel, Jorge Hardoy, and Nora Scott Kinzer (The Hague: Mouton, 1978); John Stuart MacDonald, "Planning Implementation and Social Policy: An Evaluation of Ciudad Guayana, 1965 and 1975," in *Progress in Planning,* ed. D. R. Diamond and J. B. McLoughlin (Elmsford, N.Y.: Pergamon Press, 1979), 11:1–211.

8. CVG, División de Estudios, Programación e Investigación, Subgerencia de Estadistica, *Estadisticas de la region Guayana* (Caracas, August 1980).

9. MacDonald, "Planning Implementation."

10. Peattie, "What to Do with Your Anthropologist," 1.

11. See Peattie, "The Sewer Controversy."

12. Lisa Peattie, "Conflicting Views of the Project: Caracas versus the Site," in *Planning Urban Growth and Regional Development,* by Lloyd Rodwin et al. (Cambridge: MIT Press, 1969), 453–64.

13. Lisa Peattie, "Preliminary Listing of Existing and Incipient 'Social Problems' (*sic*) on the Site" (Joint Center Guayana Project, Memorandum C-25, May 24, 1963).

14. Lisa Peattie, "Notes on Questions Put Forward by Appleyard in Memo of December 1962" (Joint Center Guayana Project, Memorandum C-24, May 22, 1963), 2–3.

15. Lisa Peattie, "Plan for a Social Study of the San Félix–Puerto Ordaz Area" (Joint Center Guayana Project, Memorandum C-23, March 17, 1962).

16. Lisa Peattie, "Some Notes on 'Social Planning' in the Guayana Project" (Joint Center Guayana Project, Memorandum C-10, June 20, 1962), 1.

17. Roderick and Lisa Peattie, "Planning Problems" (Joint Center Guayana Project, Memorandum E-26, May 15, 1962), 1.

18. Peattie, "Some Notes on 'Social Planning,' " 3.

19. Lisa Peattie, "Notes on the Lerner Memorandum" (Joint Center Guayana Project, Memorandum C-11, July 1, 1962), 1.

20. Pablo Neruda, *Bestiary,* trans. Elsa Neuberger (New York: Harcourt Brace Jovanovich, 1965).

21. Lisa Redfield Peattie, *The View from the Barrio* (Ann Arbor: University of Michigan Press, 1968).

22. Pitkin, "The Concept of Representation," 17.

23. Ibid., 20–21.

24. Castañeda and de Cesaris, "Movimientos vecinales."

25. See Lisa Redfield Peattie, "Social Structure and Social Action," chap. 6 in *The View from the Barrio* (Ann Arbor: University of Michigan Press, 1968), 54–70.

26. Pitkin, "The Concept of Representation," 20.

27. Ibid., 6.

Chapter 7

The Production of False Consciousness

To review what we know already of the outcome of the Guayana Project: The city as implemented falls considerably short of the hopes held out for it by its planners. It is smaller and lacks some of the hoped-for industrial development. It is still very much a creature of its development agency, rather than normalized through the transfer of responsibility to standard governmental and private management. Instead of having its population more or less equally distributed on the west and east sides of the Caroní River, three-quarters live to the east; given the location of industry on the west, this provides for an enormously inefficient commuting pattern. Both sides of the city lack amenity, although they are disagreeable in different ways—the west for its impersonality and lack of collective activities and lack of places to carry on such activities, the east for its disorderly shacks and lack of services. There is a high degree of social inequality in the city; in this the city does not differ from Venezuela as a whole, but more than is usual in Venezuela this is expressed in sharp spatial separation between rich and poor, and the inequality is thus even more than usually visible. The combination of the spatial separation and social polarization makes what is certainly in a functional sense a single city appear as two distinct social worlds. Thus it is only the planners who know their product as "Ciudad Guayana"; in the telephone directory, ticket agency, and common conversation it appears as distinct settlements, two cities.

How should we appraise this outcome of the highly publicized planning process? How could this outcome have been improved?

One way of dealing with these issues of evaluation is to set the question of the quality of the city rather to one side and to focus instead on the degree to which the planning seems to have been instrumental in making something happen. This is, in fact, a common approach. Indeed, when one discusses the Guayana Project and its outcome with planners who were not involved in the project a frequent comment is: "Well, anyhow, something got built." One is reminded here of the profession's experiences with "paper plans": plans which were never implemented at all. A review of four new towns planned in Venezuela during the sixties reports that of the four, Ciudad Guayana was the only one in which something really got built.[1]

We are being told that it is to the credit of the planners that they facilitated actual building—even if the form of the built environment that was the outcome of the planning process bears a rather loose relationship to that proposed in the plan.

What we learn from this, I think is that one of the ways in which planning is judged is on its capacity to mobilize capital. One might argue as to whether the resulting investment is a good one or a bad one, whether it is in the right place or the wrong place, whether it is humanely or inhumanely executed—but at least, we say, "something got built."

If we follow this train of thought, we may soon find ourselves taking the somewhat cynical position which turns the sequence from planning to implementation on its head and proposes that it is the hoped-for projects of execution which in fact drive planning. In this view, planning is an umbrella of coordination and legitimation for projects. If projects are the outcome of the plans it is not because the planners thought them up in the course of planning as a way of realizing their general objectives; they were there all along, hiding under the planning process. The general objectives are secondary, rationalizations.

Let us recall that some people—participants in the Guayana Project with a reasonable claim to knowledge—believe that

Colonel Ravard's central purpose was the building of the Guri Dam. He wanted the World Bank to finance the dam, and he needed the aluminum company and the city to legitimize the project. If this is correct, the goals of industrial growth, regional development, and decentralization were secondary to the particular objective of executing the dam. The program was project-driven.

Upon reflection, we have every reason to expect that the large comprehensive planning project will turn out, on close inspection, to be driven by a particular project or projects. It has been pointed out that the larger the group to be benefited by a particular outcome the less likely it is for the group to undertake collective action to further its ends, whereas a small group sharing a common interest is quite likely to go after it.[2] A "project" represents exactly such a structure of interest for some group—or groups—whether it be builders, users, or even planners or political sponsors. Thus a comprehensive plan may perhaps best be thought about as a cluster of projects, coordinated and rationalized under the umbrella of planning. The efforts of the Guayana Project economists to attract industry to the site may be understood not so much as the furtherance of national goals as the effort to attract special interests to move an enterprise which had its origin in Ravard's wish for the dam; and the activity of planning the city may be considered the particular project of the planners themselves.

Switching to the issue of quality of outcome, it is also possible to look at the plan as a product in itself: Was this a good plan that was—unfortunately—not well implemented? The chief designer of the Joint Center team, Wilhelm von Moltke, for example, is happy with the way the "cul-de-sac" urbanizations turned out but distressed by the environment produced by the high-rise apartment blocks on the west side of the Caroní.

We had always visualized that construction in this area would not exceed five floors. We did not bother to specify this height limitation because of lack of development pressure and becauseexperts had assured us that the soil could not support any higher structures. On a recent visit I discovered to my dismay that the Center had been Manhattanized. The land use plan and the street alignments follow our 1964 plan, but a good number of the lots support high-rise buildings, changing the overall density and the definition of the public space.

In separating "planning" from "execution" it is possible for von Moltke's summation to describe the ways in which it was "impossible to implement elements at the right time" and to find that "despite these difficulties, the resulting over-all plan is well suited to the constraints and opportunities of the situation. . . . Ciudad Guayana will develop a memorable image that will be an inspiration to the inhabitant and visitor alike."[3]

The account of the Guayana Project presented here does not separate "plan" from "implementation." The city where the Caroní joins the Orinoco is not just as the planners proposed it. But the account here argues that it is the outcome of their planning. The city with its inequality, its lack of amenity, and its striking division between rich and poor was produced by a set of processes in which planning played a conspicuous role. How, then, could the planners have improved the outcome?

With the wisdom of hindsight it is possible to imagine that things could have been made somewhat different by having more of the planning of the city go on at the site. This would have meant primarily the Joint Center staff; they had less to lose than the Venezuelans in personal and professional contacts in Caracas, and what they lost in interaction with their Venezuelan counterparts they would, I believe, have made up in the leverage of knowing more about what was actually going on.

Working on the site would have changed the planning process. The planners would have been more aware of process and timing; they would have focused less on the design of forms and more on controls and incentives. As a result, the designed forms would have been better implemented; they would have been unlikely to have let the Center disappear in problems of timing and negotiation. Perhaps they would have found ways to locate more of the population on the west side of the Caroní. Planning would have been more realistic and implementation more skillful; the present city would come closer to the plan for it.

Working on the site would have altered the politics of planning. Living on the site, the planners would have been more accessible to pressure from the people on the site and would have shaped programs to meet those needs. For example, there would almost certainly have been more concern with an acceptable format for incremental building areas on the west side of the city. Economic planning would probably have paid more attention to enterprises producing for a local market, and there would have been at least some attempt to develop industries employing the unskilled and women. There would surely have been an interest in local agriculture; for to people living and working in the city it would have seemed absurd to ship food from the coast when market gardeners in the region had no way of getting their food to the city market and no incentive to produce more.

But location would not have altered the politics of planning very much. The initiative for the Guayana Project came from Caracas, and the interests that drove it were based in Caracas and in its elites. This is the case whether one interprets the enterprise as one serving national goals of industrial growth and decentralization, or as centered on Ravard's interest in promoting the Guri Dam. In either case, the interests of people at the site had to give way. The basing of planning in Caracas followed the logic of the project itself. If some planning had been done on the site, it would only have modified the situation marginally. It would not have been possible to transfer the operation as a whole to the Guayana; and to propose that the plan should serve the interest of the poor, other than through the logic of trickle-down, would have been

like whistling for water to run uphill; there was nothing in the
politics of the time to push it there.

One way to look at the outcome of the Guayana Project is as
a manifestation of the contradictions between what Marxists see
as the two major functions of the state: accumulation and legitimization. In the words of James O'Connor:

> Our first premise is that the capitalistic state must try to fulfill
> two basic and often mutually contradictory functions—*accu-
> mulation* and *legitimization*. This means that the state must try
> to maintain or create the conditions in which profitable capital
> accumulation is possible. However, the state also must try to
> maintain or create the conditions for social harmony.

These functions compete or conflict.

> A capitalist state that openly uses its coercive forces to help
> one class accumulate capital at the expense of other classes loses
> its legitimacy and hence undermines the basis of its loyalty and
> support. But a state that ignores the necessity of assisting the
> process of capital accumulation risks drying up the source of
> its own power, the economy's surplus production capacity and
> the taxes drawn from this surplus (and other forms of capital).
> . . . The state must involve itself in the accumulation process,
> but it must either mystify its policies by calling them some-
> thing that they are not or it must try to conceal them (e.g., by
> making them into administrative, not political, issues.)[4]

The Guayana Project was a project centered on capitalist accumulation: its purpose was to reorganize the region to serve the
interests of corporate investors. The fact that—so far as we can
discern—the corporate investors were not pushing the enterprise,
but in fact had to be lured to take part, does not weaken this point
but only adds salience to the issue. One need not see the CVG

as handmaid to capitalism (roughly, O'Connor's view); the situation is the same if the state is seen as a relatively independent cluster of institutions. In any event, the CVG needed the corporate resources to build its institutional empire. The way to attract corporate participation was to construct an environment around the needs of the corporations.

But to serve the purpose of legitimization, that effort to reorganize the environment for the corporations had to be made to appear as a work of general social betterment. The task of planning was to integrate accumulation and legitimization in a single set of projects. Guayana had to serve both purposes and to represent both symbolically as a kind of embodiment of the ideas of modernity and progress which, on an ideological level, fused the two. One can see the whole planning enterprise and the various forms of representation employed within it as a not wholly successful attempt at reconciling accumulation and legitimization.

Some consequences of the contradictions between accumulation and legitimization were quite troublesome. The contradictions were embedded, very visibly, in the physical form of the city itself. The aim of attracting corporate investment implied a large industrial area with central facilities like a port. It also suggested high-standard residential areas for employees of the corporations. At the same time, the legitimization function required that this reorganization of the environment, via public powers and public funds, for the advantage of rich corporations and their privileged employees, had to be projected as a project for the general social welfare—"progress." This interpretation was presented in various written documents, but another of the means selected was the use of the city itself as physical symbol of the idea of progress; the city had to have the physical appearance of affluent modernity.

The problem was, who should pay for the city of affluent modernity? The state development corporation was ready to erect icons of modernity here and there; it built its administration building and its avenue, and later, even as a bitter strike of the workers of the steel mill was exploding, asked one of the designers to investigate the possibility of placing fountains in the center of the major traffic interchanges. But it was certainly not prepared to give to any major part of the workers of the city the kinds of modern housing or infrastructure that the imagery of progress seemed to imply. At the same time, it could certainly not be imagined that the wages paid in the new industries would be such as to permit the workers to build or buy such modern housing for themselves; that would be to defeat the basic purpose of capitalist accumulation.

The solution found was spatial segregation. One part of the city became the showcase: the city of affluent modernity. Here were the major industries, the central building of the development agency, the prestige retail firms, the elite urbanizations for high-level personnel, and the towers of high-rent condominiums. Although with some reluctance a couple of urbanizations were eventually developed for "lower-income" families, these still had to be of a standard which made them inaccessible to most of the population; shanties were to be forbidden. On the other side of the river, the majority of the population, only very modestly served by funding for roads and water lines, housed themselves as best they might—largely in a spread of unserviced shantytowns.

The city had thus become—visually, although of course not functionally—two cities: that on the west, the city of affluent modernity, could appear as the "planned city"; that on the east, the city of shantytowns, could appear as "lack of planning." (It may be recalled that this was the way my cab driver saw things.) The public bodies that created the inequality by treating the two sides differently could thus be seen as getting the credit for the world of the "haves" while avoiding blame for the world of the have-nots.

But in many ways, this solution has served neither accumulation nor legitimization very well. The cost in economic efficiency is obvious; the majority of the workers have a very long commute over a route which bottlenecks at the bridges. The cost of commuting is charged against the price of steel. On the other hand, the outcome has also done badly for legitimization. The physical form of the city dramatizes the contrast in living standards and in public provision between the elite groups and the mass of the population. Disraeli looked in the streets of London and saw mingled there "two Englands." The Venezuelan social critic sees two cities, one of the rich and one of the poor, confronting each other on the opposite banks of the Caroní, and photographs of these contrasts illustrate journalism on the "social problem" in Guayana.

But in some respects the joining of accumulation and legitimization in the Guayana Project worked quite well. The idea of high-technology corporate investment as the vehicle of general social progress was at the time very little questioned. Some of the participants argued that there should be more attention to the generation of employment; some people worried particularly about jobs for women, considering the number of female-headed households. One of the economists on the Joint Center team made himself thought of as something of a crank by recurrently raising the issue of regional development in agriculture. But the general idea of corporatized industrial growth and its support by general funds being a desirable programmatic approach was acceded to by elite technocrat and poor shantytown dweller alike.

When James O'Connor goes on to describe the conflicts between accumulation and legitimization in the United States of America in the 1960s we see an account of a system in which legitimization came a great deal harder than it did in Venezuela at the time of the Guayana Project. The American state is seen operating a complex and expensive welfare system designed, in O'Connor's view, "chiefly to keep social peace among unemployed workers," and in the complicated political task of designing and getting passed a tax system which benefits business while appearing as progressive. The Venezuelan state at the time of the Guayana Project had few of these problems. Oil revenues kept the money coming in without the necessity of building a more complex system of taxation, and the trickle-down of oil prosperity in itself tended to legitimize the vision of progress. In the world of belief in progress, there appeared to be little need to legitimize aid to industry by add-ons of social programming or ideological reasoning; industry was its own legitimization. The planners who spoke of "growth poles" at the top of the system were echoed by my acquaintance in the dusty chinos who waved in the direction of the steel mill and said, "Industry is the future of the worker."

For the project to develop as it did, however, accumulation and legitimization had to be fused not only at the level of ideology but at the level of practice. The idea of progress via corporate investment had to be grounded in the professional practice of the planners and in the institutional context within which that practice took place.

At this point the analysis of the planning enterprise in terms of Marxist functionalism and the theory of the state meets with the analysis of planning as the rationale for projects. "The state" is an abstraction; at the operational level, we must understand why particular divisions and the employees who staff them behave as they do. One part of the Guayana Project story is the understanding of the planning profession and its conventions of practice at the beginning of the sixties. For while we might reasonably think of planning as an instrument by which the state exercises its functions of accumulation and legitimization, it does not follow from this that planners, as real-life people, are tools to be commanded to exercise these functions. Instead, for the state to function as O'Connor says it does it must be the case that particular people, such as in this case planners, see it as an interesting and professionally gratifying project to carry out an enterprise which has the outcome identified. And here we see that through a historical process which we certainly will not take time to trace here the conventions of planning practice were such as to serve the purpose of legitimizing a project which had as its primary purpose the transfer of resources to large corporations and their well-to-do staffs.

In focusing, earlier, on the way in which reality was represented in the planning process, I have tried to point out that the organization of the planning enterprise and the techniques used for planning were well adapted to the purpose of hiding issues of distribution and of the political and social quality of the city to be produced by the project. The economic program was treated as the "basis," setting the parameters for city planning; this insured that the needs of the corporations were treated as primary. The participation of urban designers and social researchers were to insure that human needs would be met and social problems addressed; thus there appeared to be no need to enter into the contentious realm of claim and counterclaim or, indeed, to consult the various groups who might be involved in the city. Within each specialization in the planning team, conventional professional practice contributed to the legitimizing outcome. The process for the economists was to begin with a wish list of industries and build the population and spatial structure of the city out from that; it would have seemed to them an exercise in fantasy—and it would certainly have lacked legitimacy to the CVG—had they begun by describing the nature of economic activity to support some ideal city. The process for social researchers like myself was to ascertain "needs" and study problems; when I expressed indignation with some CVG policy or proposed a different way of interacting with the citizenry I was seen as stepping out of the professional role. The urban designers saw it as their role to translate the requirements of efficiency and the needs of people into design; in the process, there was little or no attention to conflicting interests in the built environment and the way in which the development of the city benefited some and disadvantaged others.

The legitimacy of these forms of professional practice was in turn protected by political institutions which represented local interest at a very local level—that of community projects—and kept larger issues to be settled in the technocratic politics of the ministries and agencies in Caracas. The forms of representation in planning technique were congruent with the political forms of representation. There was no set of political leaders prepared to take a local grievance about a sewage outlet on my beach and generalize it into a complaint against a development agency which would build such a project and the pattern of development which put the needs of the well-to-do for sewage disposal above the needs of the poor for clean water.

Ideology, planning practice, and political institutions supported each other. The system worked because the oil money and the recency and rapidity of the changes it had brought made economic growth appear both possible and desirable. Accumulation and legitimization were joined in a way which may never happen so smoothly again.

The economist Albert Hirschman has written that

> in the early stages of rapid economic development when inequalities in the distribution of income between different classes, sectors and regions are apt to increase sharply, it can happen that society's *tolerance* for such disparities will also increase. To the extent that this greater tolerance comes into being, it accommodates, as it were, the increasing inequalities in an almost providential fashion.[5]

The Venezuelan case is a splendid example of growing inequality combined with a great tolerance for inequality. The brief summary of recent Venezuelan history with which we began this account should have suggested some of the reasons why there should be tolerance of inequality. The burst of new opportunities under the oil boom had made the people at the bottom of the system enormously sanguine as to the future possibilities for themselves and their children. Hirschman develops this theme in an analogy:

> Suppose I drive through a two-lane tunnel, both lanes going in the same direction, and run into a serious traffic jam. No car moves in either lane as far as I can see (which is not very far). I am in the left lane and feel dejected. After a while, the cars in the right lane begin to move. Naturally, my spirits lift considerably, for I know that the jam has broken and that my lane's turn to move will surely come any moment now. Even though I still sit still, I feel much better off than before because of the expectation that I shall soon be on the move.

But, Hirschman says, this tolerance is like a credit that falls due at a certain date. "It is extended in the expectation that eventually the disparities will narrow again." His analogy continues:

> But suppose the expectation is disappointed and only the right lane keeps moving: in that case I, along with my left lane co-sufferers, shall suspect foul play, and many of us will at some point become quite furious and ready to correct manifest injustice by taking direct action (such as illegally crossing the double line separating the two lanes).[6]

Hirschman goes on to speculate as to the conditions that govern the timing of this hypothetical turnaround time, the time when the credit falls due. Here, when we try to move from the fable to the real world, we see at once how the story simplifies. In the real world many more variables enter than in the simplified two-lane tunnel of the fable. Do those whose progress is arrested feel things are being competently managed and that eventually the competent authorities will fix things up? Or do they deeply distrust the managers of the system for other reasons? Under what conditions do those whose progress is slow or negligible tend still to feel some kinship or identification with those who are getting ahead faster? How do people measure their progress, anyhow? Does everyone feel that they are moving on the same path as everyone else? For surely there is also the South African system in which pains are taken to try to keep some people from entering the tunnel at all.

Many or most of these conditions must of course have to do with the basic structure of the economy and the sorts of political and social interest organizations which get developed in the early stage. But it must be also somewhat governed by forces of ideology—those systems of ideas which every modern society develops to bridge the disparity of interests and to mobilize action within a single national framework.

Planning seems to be important in these issues, for planning not only relates to the world of traffic management—which lanes get kept open and which are blocked—but also to the world of explanation and understanding. In planning, accumulation and legitimization are brought together within a single set of activities which must somehow accommodate their discrepancies. The specifics of how this is managed must vary with time and circumstances. The circumstances of the Guayana Project varied even within the span of our story; planning in the service of project promotion at the beginning was quite different from planning as a vehicle of interaction with the local citizenry twenty years later. Venezuela when the oil money was rolling and the idea of development had its full luster was a special time which will probably not be repeated. The atmosphere, with the general enthusiasm for "progress," made it almost impossible to question a kind of planning, and of representing reality, which submerged issues of inequality and conflicts of interest under the imagery of a glamorized modernity.

Indeed, looking back at the Guayana Project with the twenty-twenty vision of hindsight, we can see that the intellectual framework and techniques of representation used by the planners obscured not only the issues of distribution but also potential issues of purpose and social goals. In fact we can see that the Marxist analysis of James O'Connor shares with the planners of Guayana a set of underlying assumptions which are now not quite so self-evident as they were then. O'Connor's distinction between accumulation and legitimization is the counterpart to the planners' distinction between economic issues and "the social part." Both distinctions reflect a common belief that economic issues are somehow more real and more basic than social ones. Both O'Connor and the Guayana planners see economic output as measurable, economic interests as objectively real, economic conditions as shaping social ones, goals and values as taking form in a world of hard practical fact.

This kind of economism is also, now, somewhat under question. Along with a weakening of faith in progress have come a number of ideas and social movements—ecology, feminism, "Green politics"—which treat the quality of life as being as central to political purpose as material goods and the distribution of material goods. Such movements often do not make a clear separation between "the economy" and "the social part" but deal instead in concepts like "right livelihood."

On a theoretical level, the anthropologist Marshall Sahlins has looked at the conventional opposition between "culture" and "practical reason" and concluded that material needs and means—the subject matter we call "economic"—are given by cultural selection and definition rather than by the order of nature. "Practical reason" and the idea of the economic are cultural phenomena. Indeed, for Sahlins, the very idea of the economic is a central cultural production of the capitalist society of his time. "But if our own economy does not elude the human condition, if capitalism too is a symbolic process, wherein lies the uniqueness of Western 'civilization'?" he asks, and answers: "Perhaps in nothing so much as the illusion that it is otherwise—that the economy and society are pragmatically constructed." In extending this view, he provides a context for Ciudad Guayana.

> For us the production of goods is at the same time the privileged mode of symbolic production and transmission. The uniqueness of bourgeois society consists not in the fact that the economic system escapes symbolic determination, but that the economic symbolism is structurally determining.[7]

Suppose that Ciudad Guayana had been planned in an era in which Sahlins's view had been general. Suppose that its planners had seen it as the centerpiece of an idea of economic progress that was itself open to question, one vision among many competing human visions. That is not yet our current condition. But if movements which question our general goals grow and cumulate in our political and intellectual life it will be much less obvious than it was in the sixties that planning properly begins with goals of "economic growth" and then adds "social aspects." There will then be a new set of tasks set for representation.

One of the comments which present-day planners often make on the Guayana Project story is: "Oh, that was fifties planning." The focus on "the plan" as product, the outcome of a comprehensive planning process taking into account both the various technical components and the social groups of the city was, indeed, state-of-the-art planning at the time. It would not be so today. With the sixties there came into vogue in the U.S. planning profession a different view of planning. This view confronted diverse and competing interests and attempted to harmonize them by representation and negotiation rather than by having the planners identify and plan *for* the diversity. It became common to speak of planning as process rather than as product.

This contrast reconfirms the basic importance of politics. The new styles of planning that came into use in the sixties, and the views of profession and of society they embody, came into existence through an era of intense political struggle around planning issues. These struggles, in turn, came about through the intersection, in a particular period of time, of a specific set of historic forces. The federally funded redevelopment and highway programs of the sixties proposed to displace from the city slums groups of people whose neighborhood organization was simultaneously being funded through the War on Poverty and whose militance was sparked by the civil rights and black power movements. Meanwhile, the New Left's focus on democratizing the institutions attached itself especially to the transformation of professional practice, and groups of young planners, like groups of young doctors and lawyers, tried to find ways to turn their professional skills to working with "the people."

Citizens disrupted meetings and sat down in front of the bulldozers. Professionals experimented with "advocacy planning" and "community design." The rules and procedures of city building came to incorporate a variety of structures for citizen participation: advocacy, public hearings, community boards, impact statements.

As has been mentioned, some of these institutions have come into existence in Ciudad Guayana. There are the neighborhood committees, the commission on zoning, the conservation board. In the Venezuelan national planning body, there has been a move to replace "normative planning," which assumes that only the state makes plans and that plans are based on consensus, by a "situational or strategic planning" which takes political actors into account.[8] In part, the creation of these institutions responds to political movements within Venezuela, both at the grassroots and at the national level. But their creation is also in part a response to the American example. Social inventions diffuse as technical ones do. When the present-day planner in the CVG office told me he thought of himself as a "guerrilla in the bureaucracy," he was referring to a book by that title published in the States in the sixties dealing with the activities of radical planners in New York.

These social inventions comprise both a body of social institutions and a body of organizational techniques which change the nature of politics in an incremental way. For example, as has been mentioned, the intensity of the urban struggles in the United States in the sixties is explained in part by the organization building that was part of the War on Poverty. Resistance to slum clearance could draw not only on established institutions like the Catholic church with its need to defend the integrity of the parish, but on the new antipoverty organizations and the social workers whose salaries were drawn there. Planners learned how to work with organizers. Programmatic descriptions represent reality as problem, process, community, and group. In 1982 a planner in Venezuela tries to understand the potentialities of his role by comparing his work to that of planners in the New York City system earlier. Both institution creating and technique development, taken together, have been thought of as social learning, in a view which sees in politics not simply the ebb and flow of power struggles or the inexorable unfolding of the logic of history, but some kind of cumulative social progress, built by people.

In the era of the military-industrial complex, the growth of nuclear arms stockpiles, and international interventions by the industrial powers, it is hard to construe the general movement of human history as social learning. But somewhere within these movements of power—and the planning which goes into them— there is also a struggle for a social learning how to build a humane world which continues to attract idealistic young people both into issue politics and into the field of planning.

For planners who come after, the Guayana Project seems to hold three general lessons. One is antitechnical, one focuses on professional technique, and the third in some sense links the first two.

The first lesson is that the planner cannot will a world into existence. Planning does not carry its own power. The planner must ally with individuals, institutions, and social forces in the world out there. The choice of where to make these alliances is not free, in the sense of being unconstrained, but choice is possible.

The second lesson is that the techniques of planning are not neutral. Every way of representing the world implies one perspective among other possible perspectives and serves some interests better than others. The planner who wants to ally with some group or interest cannot simply adopt a set of techniques and forms of representation developed in the context of a *different* social placement and set of alliances, but must rethink the technical issues afresh.

The third lesson is that the sophisticated professional planner will understand practice as a form of action embedded in society and having a time dimension, part of the complex and continuing processes by which we create a world which is both material and meaningful.

Notes

1. Alan Turner, "New Towns in the Developing World: Three Case Studies," in *International Urban Growth Policies: New Town Contributions,* ed. Gideon Golany (New York: John Wiley and Sons, 1978), 249–76.
2. Mancur Olson, Jr., *The Logic of Collective Action: Public Goods and the Theory of Groups* (Cambridge: Harvard University Press, 1965).
3. Von Moltke, "Urban Design Intent," 123–24 and 84–85.
4. James O'Connor, *The Fiscal Crisis of the State* (New York: St. Martin's Press, 1973), 6.
5. Albert Hirschman, "The Changing Tolerance for Income Inequality in the Course of Economic Development," *Quarterly Journal of Economics* 87, no. 3 (August 1973): 545.
6. Ibid.
7. Marshall Sahlins, *Culture and Practical Reason* (Chicago: University of Chicago Press, 1976), 210–11.
8. María-Pilar García, letter to author, June 11, 1985.

Index